The Book Of This And That

By

Robert Lynd

The Book Of This And That
by Robert Lynd

Copyright © 2023

All Rights reserved.

ISBN: 978-93-60465-79-7
Published by

DOUBLE 9 BOOKS

2/13-B, Ansari Road
Daryaganj, New Delhi – 110002
info@double9books.com
www.double9books.com
Tel. 011-40042856

ABOUT THE AUTHOR

Robert Wilson Lynd was an Irish author who lived from April 20, 1879, to October 6, 1949. He edited poetry, wrote literary essays, was a socialist, and was an Irish patriot. A Presbyterian minister named Robert John Lynd and his wife Sarah Rentoul Lynd had Lynd at 3 Brookhill Avenue in Cliftonville, Belfast. She was the second of seven children. Lynd's great-grandfather on his dad's side moved from Scotland to Ireland. Lynd went to school at the Royal Belfast Academical Institution and made friends with James Winder Good and Paul Henry. He then went to Queen's University to study. His father was a Presbyterian Church Moderator for a while. He was the second in a long line of Presbyterian pastors in the family. An essayist who wrote about Lynd in 2003 said that his "maternal grandfather, great-grandfather, and great-great-grandfather had all been Presbyterian clergymen." Lynd started out as a reporter on The Northern Whig in Belfast, working with James Winder Good. He went to London from Manchester in 1901 and shared a house with Paul Henry, who was already a well-known artist. First, he wrote about theater for Today, which was edited by Jerome K. Jerome. He also wrote for the Daily News (later the News Chronicle), and from 1912 to 1947, he was the literary editor of that paper.

CONTENTS

I   SUSPICION 7

II   ON GOOD RESOLUTIONS 11

III   THE SIN OF DANCING 15

IV   THOUGHTS AT A TANGO TEA 19

V   THE HUMOURS OF MURDER 23

VI   THE DECLINE AND FALL OF HELL 28

VII   ON CHEERFUL READERS 32

VIII   ST G. B. S. AND THE BISHOP 36

IX   STUPIDITY 40

X   WASTE 44

XI   ON CHRISTMAS 48

XII   ON DEMAGOGUES 52

XIII   ON COINCIDENCES 56

XIV   ON INDIGNATION 60

XV   THE HEART OF MR GALSWORTHY 64

XVI   SPRING FASHIONS 68

XVII   ON BLACK CATS 72

XVIII   ON BEING SHOCKED 76

XIX   CONFESSIONS 80

XX   THE TERRORS OF POLITICS 84

XXI   ON DISASTERS 88

XXII   THE RIGHTS OF MURDER 92

XXIII   THE HUMOUR OF HOAXES 96

XXIV   ANATOLE FRANCE 100

XXV   THE SEA 104

XXVI   THE FUTURISTS 109

XXVII   A DEFENCE OF CRITICS 113

XXVIII   ON THE BEAUTY OF STATISTICS 117

I
SUSPICION

Suspicion is a beast with a thousand eyes, but most of them are blind, or colour-blind, or askew, or rolling, or yellow. It is a beast with a thousand ears, but most of them are like the ears of the deaf man in the comic recitation who, when you say "whiskers" hears "solicitors," and when you are talking about the weather thinks you are threatening to murder him. It is a beast with a thousand tongues, and they are all slanderous. On the whole, it is the most loathsome monster outside the pages of *The Faërie Queene*. Just as the ugliest ape that ever was born is all the more repellent for being so like a man, so suspicion is all the more hideous because it is so close a caricature of the passion for truth. It is a leering perversion of that passion which sent Columbus looking for a lost continent and urged Galileo to turn his telescope on the heavens. Columbus may, in a sense, be said to have suspected that America was there, and Galileo suspected more than was good for his comfort about the conduct of the stars. But these were noble suspicions—leaps into the light. They are no more comparable to the suspicions which are becoming a feature of public life than the energies of an explorer of the South Pole are comparable to the energies of one of those private detectives who are paid to grub after evidence in divorce cases. One might put it a good deal more strongly, indeed, for the private detective may in his own way be an officer of truth and humanity, while the suspicious politician is the prophet only of party disreputableness. He is like the average suspicious husband, in the case of whom, even when his suspicions are true, one is inclined to sympathise with the wife for being married to so green-eyed a fool. Suspicion, take it all in all, is the most tedious and scrannel of the sins.

It would be folly, of course, to suggest that there is no such thing as justifiable suspicion. If you see a man in a Tube lift with his hand on some old gentleman's watch-chain, you are justified in suspecting that his object is something less innocent than to persuade the old gentleman to become a Plymouth Brother. But the man of suspicious temperament is not content with cases of this sort. He is the sort of man who, if it were not for the law of libel, would suspect the Rev. F. B. Meyer of having stolen La Gioconda from the Louvre.

His suspicions are like those of a man who would accost you in the street with the assertion that you had just murdered the President of the United States or that you were hiding a stolen Dreadnought in your pocket. Obviously there would be no reply to a man like this, except that he was mad. He has got an idea into his head, and it is his idea, and not the proof or disproof that the idea has any justification, which seems to him to be the most important thing in the world. Suspicion, indeed, is a well-known form of mania. Husbands suspect their wives of trying to poison their beer; friends suspect friends of planning the most extraordinary series of losses and humiliations for them. Nothing can happen but the suspicious man believes that somebody did it on purpose. He is like the savage who cannot believe that his great-grandmother died without somebody having plotted it. Obviously, to believe things like this is to put poison in the air, and it is not surprising to learn that the savage goes out and murders the first man he meets for being his great-grandmother's murderer. In this matter civilised man is little better than the savage. He knows a little more about natural laws, and so he is not suspicious of quite the same things; but his suspicions, as soon as he begins to harbour them, swiftly strip off his civilisation as a drunken man strips off his coat in order to fight in the street. He becomes Othello while the clock is striking. Straightway, all the world's his bolster; there is no creature on earth so innocent or so beautiful that he will not smother it in the insanity of his passion. Literature is to a great extent an indictment of suspicion. *The Ring and the Book* is an epic of suspicion, and the *Blot on the 'Scutcheon* is its tragedy. In the story of Paolo and Francesca, again, we are made feel that the hideous thing was not the love of Paolo and Francesca, but the murderous suspicion of Malatesta. In this case it may be admitted, there was justice in the suspicion; but suspicion is so very loathsome a thing that, even when it is just, we like it as little as we like spying. All we can say in its favour is that it is more pitiable. Men do not go spying because there is a fury in their bosoms, but the suspicious man is one who is being eaten alive at the heart. He wears the mark of doom on his sullen brows as surely as Cain. For such a man the sun does not shine and the stars are silver conspirators. He is a person who can suspect whole landscapes; he sees a countryside, not as an exciting pattern of meadow and river-bend and hills and smoke among trees, but as an arrangement of a thousand farms with fierce dogs eager for the calves of his legs. He can concentrate his affections on nothing beautiful. He can see only worms in buds. He can ultimately follow nothing with enthusiasm but will-o'-the-wisps. To go after these he will leave wife and children and lands, and he will dance into the perils of the marshes, into sure drowning—a lost figure of derision or pity, according to your gentleness.

Nor is it only in private life that suspicion is a light that leads men into bog-holes. Suspicion in public life is also a disaster among passions. Englishmen who realise this must have noticed with apprehension the growth of suspicion as a principle in recent years.

Suspicion is the arch-calumniator. That is why, of all weapons, it is most avoided by decent fighters. Every honourable man would rather be calumniated than a calumniator—every sensible man, too, for calumny is the worst policy. It is clear that while the public men of a country are prepared to believe each other capable of anything there can be no more national unity than in present-day Mexico or than in Poland before the partition. It is the same with parties as with nations. The reason why revolutionary parties are so rarely successful is that the members suspect not only everybody else but each other. The more revolutionary the party is, the more the members are inclined to regard each other, not as potential Garibaldis, but potential traitors. For much the same reasons criminal conspiracies seldom prosper. Crime seems to create an atmosphere of suspicion, and co-operation among men who doubt each other is impossible. But it is the same with every conspiracy, whether it is criminal or not. Secrecy seems to awaken all the nerves of suspicion, even when one is secret for the public good, and the conspirators soon find themselves believing the most ludicrous things. Who has not known committees on which some man or woman will not sit because of an idea that some other member is in the pay of Scotland Yard? The amusing part of the business is that this kind of thing goes on even in committees about the proceedings of which there is no need of secrecy at all and at which reporters from the *Times* might be present for all the harm to man or beast that is discussed. But there is a tradition of suspicion in some movements that serves the purpose of enabling many innocent people to lead exciting lives. I once knew a man who spent half his time tying up his bootlaces under lamp-posts. He had an invincible belief that detectives followed him, and he was never content till he had allowed whoever was behind him to get past. Scotland Yard, I am confident, knew as little of him as it does of Wordsworth. But it was his folly to think otherwise, and for all I know he may be going on with those slow but sensational walks of his through the London streets at the present day. This is the amusing side of suspicion. Unfortunately, it has also its base and mirthless side. Practically, every bloody mistake—I use the word not as an oath—in the French Revolution was the result of suspicion. It began with suspicion of the Girondins; but suspicion of Danton and Robespierre soon followed. Suspicion is a monster that devours her own children. Manifestly, no movement can succeed in which men believe that their friends are viler than their enemies. But in every movement, there are men who make a trade of suspecting the leaders in their own camp, and the Socialist movement is as much exposed to the plague as any other. Suspicion of this kind, I think, is a bitter form of egoism. It is a trampling of the suspected persons under one's own white feet.

Nor is it only in movements and in nations that suspicion plays havoc. International suspicion is a no less costly visitor. We live in a world in which every cup of tea we drink and every pipe of tobacco we smoke pays toll to this ancient and gluttonous dragon. Every year each country sets up huge altars of men and ships and guns to the beast, but he is not satisfied. He demands universal power, and insists that we shall give all our goods to him except just enough to keep ourselves alive and that we shall not shrink even from offering up human sacrifices at a nod of his head. Perhaps some day a new St George will arise and release us from so shameful a subjection. Common sense seems to have as little force against him as an ordinary foot-soldier against Goliath. We feel the need of some miraculous personage to put an end to our distress. Meanwhile, one may hail as prophetic the continual organisation of new knighthoods for the Suppression of the Dragon.

II
ON GOOD RESOLUTIONS

There is too little respect paid to the good resolutions which are so popular a feature of the New Year. We laugh at the man who is always turning over a new leaf as though he were the last word in absurdity, and we even invent proverbs to discourage him, such as that "the road to Hell is paved with good intentions." This makes life extremely difficult for the well-meaning. It robs many of us of the very last of our little store of virtue. Our virtue we have hitherto put almost entirely into our resolutions. To ask us to put it into our actions instead is like asking a man who has for years devoted his genius to literature to switch it off on to marine biology. Nature, unfortunately, has not made us sufficiently accommodating for these rapid changes. She has appointed to each of us his own small plot; has made one of us a poet, another an economist, another a politician—one of us good at making plans, another good at putting them into execution. One feels justified, then, in claiming for the maker of good resolutions a place in the sun. Good resolutions are too delightful a form of morality to be allowed to disappear from a world in which so much of morality is dismal. They are morality at its dawn—morality fresh and untarnished and full of song. They are golden anticipations of the day's work—anticipations of which, alas! the day's work too often proves unworthy. Work, says Amiel somewhere, is vulgarised thought. Work, I prefer to say, is vulgarised good resolutions. There are, no doubt, some people whose resolutions are so natively mediocre that it is no trouble in the world to put them into practice. Promise and performance are in such cases as like as a pair of twins; both are contemptible. But as for those of us whose promises are apt to be Himalayan, how can one expect the little pack-mule of performance to climb to such pathless and giddy heights? Are not the Himalayas in themselves a sufficiently inspiring spectacle—all the more inspiring, indeed, if some peak still remains unscaled, mysterious?

But resolutions of this magnitude belong rather to the region of day-dreams. They take one back to one's childhood, when one longed to win the football cup for one's school team, and, if possible, to have one's leg broken just as one scored the decisive try. Considering that one did not play football, this may surely be regarded as a noble example of an impossible ideal. It has the inaccessibility of a star rather than of a mountain-peak. As one grows older, one's resolutions become earthier. They are concerned with such things as giving up tobacco, taking exercise, answering letters, chewing one's food properly, going to bed before midnight, getting up before noon. This may seem a mean list enough, but there is wonderful comfort to be got out of even a modest good resolution so long as it refers, not to the next five minutes, but to to-morrow, or next week, or next month, or next year, or the year after. How vivid, how beautiful, to-morrow seems with our lordly regiment of good resolutions ready to descend upon it as upon a city seen afar off for the first time! Every day lies before us as wonderful as London lay before Blücher on the night when he exclaimed: "My God, what a city to loot!" Our life is gorgeous with to-morrows. It is all to-morrows. Good resolutions might be described, in the words in which a Cabinet Minister once described journalism, as the intelligent anticipation of events. They are, however, the intelligent anticipation of events which do not take place. They are the April of virtue with no September following.

On the other hand, there is much to be said for putting a good resolution into effect now and then. There is a brief introductory period in most human conduct, before the novelty has worn off, when doing things is almost, if not quite, as pleasant as thinking about them. Thus, if you make a resolve to get up at seven o'clock every day during the year 1915, you should do it on at least one morning. If you do, you will feel so surprised with the world, and so content with your own part in it, that you will decide to get up at seven every morning for the rest of your life. But do not be rash. Getting up early, if you do it seldom enough, is an intoxicating experience. But before long the intoxication fades, and only the habit is left. It was not the elder brother with his habits, but the prodigal with his occasional recurrence into virtue, for whom the fatted calf was killed. Even for the prodigal, when once he had settled down to orderly habits, the supply of the fatted calves from his father's farm was bound before long to come to an end.

There are, however, other good resolutions in which it is not so easy to experiment for a single morning. If you resolved to learn German, for instance, there would be very little intoxication to be got out of a single sitting face to face with a German grammar. Similarly, the inventors of systems of exercise for keeping the townsman in condition all stress the fact that, in order to attain health, one must go on toiling morning after morning at their wretched punchings and twistings and kickings till the end of time. This is an unfair advantage to take of the ordinary maker of good resolutions. He is enticed into the adventure of trying a new thing only to discover that he cannot be said to have tried it until he has tried it on a thousand occasions. Most of us, it may be said at once, are not to be enticed into such matters higher than our knees. We may go so far as to buy the latest book on health or the latest mechanical apparatus to hang on the wall. But soon they become little more than decorations for our rooms. That pair of immense dumb-bells which we got in our boyhood, when we believed that the heavier the dumb-bell the more magnificently would our biceps swell—who would think of taking them from their dusty corner now? Then there was that pair of wooden dumb-bells light as wind, which we tried for a while on hearing that heavy dumb-bells were a snare and only hardened the muscles without strengthening them. They lie now where the woodlouse may eat them if it has so lowly an appetite. But our good resolutions did really array themselves in colours when the first of the exercisers was invented. There was a thrill in those first mornings when we rose a little earlier than usual and expected to find an inch added to our chest measurement before breakfast. That is always the characteristic of good resolutions. They are founded on a belief in the possibility of performing miracles. If we could swell visibly as a result of a single half-hour's tug at weights and wires, we would all desert our morning's sleep for our exerciser with a will. But the faith that believes in miracles is an easy sort of faith. The faith that goes on believing in the final excellence, though one day shows no obvious advance on another, is the more enviable genius. It is, perhaps, the rarest thing in the world, and all the good resolutions ever made, if placed end to end, would not make so much as an inch of it. One man I knew who had faith of this kind. He used to practise strengthening his will every evening by buying almonds and raisins or some sort of sweet thing, and sitting down before them by the hour without touching them. And frequently, so he told me, he would repeat over to himself a passage which Poe quotes at the top of one of his stories—*The Fall of the House of Ussher*, was it not?—beginning "Great are the mysteries of the will." I envied him his philosophic grimness: I should never have been able to resist the almonds and raisins. But that incantation from Poe—was not that, too, but a desperate clutching after the miraculous?

There is nothing which men desire more fervently than this mighty will. It may be the most selfish or unselfish of desires. We may long for it for its own sake or for the sake of some purpose which means more to us than praise. We are eager to escape from that continuous humiliation of the promises we have made to ourselves and broken. It is all very well to talk about being baffled to fight better, but that implies a will on the heroic scale. Most of us, as we see our resolutions fly out into the sun, only to fall with broken wings before they have more than begun their journey, are inclined at times to relapse into despair. On the other hand, Nature is prodigal, and in nothing so much as good resolutions. In spite of the experience of half a lifetime of failure, we can still draw upon her for these with the excitement of faith in our hearts. Perhaps there is some instinct for perfection in us which thus makes us deny our past and stride off into the future forgetful of our chains. It is the first step that counts, says the proverb. Alas! we know that that is the step that nearly everybody can take. It is when we are about to take the steps that follow that our ankle feels the drag of old habit. For even those of us who are richest in good resolutions are the creatures of habit just as the baldly virtuous are. The only difference is that we are the slaves of old habits, while they are the masters of new ones.... On the whole, then, we cannot do better as the New Year approaches than resolve to go out once more in quest of the white flower which has already been allowed to fade too long, where Tennyson placed it, in the late Prince Consort's buttonhole.

III
THE SIN OF DANCING

It is a pleasure to see a modern clergyman expressing his horror of the dancing of the moment as Canon Newbolt did in St Paul's. One had begun to fear lately that the clergy were trying to run a race of tolerance with the dramatic critics and the nuts. On the whole I prefer clergymen in the denouncing mood. They are there to remind us that the soul does not pour out its riches in rag-time songs, that Peter is not to be bribed with trinkets, and that the gates of Heaven will not—so far as is known—open to the bark of a toy-dog. They are there, in a sentence, as the shaven critics of a saltatory world. The history of civilisation might be interpreted with some reason as a prolonged conflict between the preachers and the dancers. The preacher and the dancer may both be necessary to us, like east and west in a map; but we feel that, like east and west, they should keep their distance from each other in censorious irreconcilement. I know, of course, that the modern anthropologist is inclined to insist upon the kinship between dancing and religion. We are told that the Church was born not, it may be, under a dancing star, but at any rate under a dancing savage. The theory is that man originally expressed his deepest emotions about food, love, and war in dances. In the course of time the leaping groups felt the need of a leader, and gradually the leader of the dance evolved into a hero, or representative of the group soul, and from that he afterwards swelled into a god. This, we are asked to believe, is the lineage of Zeus. The theory strikes me as being too simple to be true. It is like an attempt to spell a long word with a single letter. At the same time, it gains colour from the fact that the heads of the Church have continually shown a tendency to dancing since the days of King David. We have it on good authority that in the Latin Church the Bishops were called Præsules because they led the dances in the church choir on feast days. It is a fact of some significance, indeed, that at more than one period of history it has been the heretics rather than the orthodox who have raged most furiously against dancing. The Albigenses and the Waldenses are both examples of this. Superficially, this may seem to weaken my contention that preaching and dancing can no more become friends than the lion and the unicorn. But, if you reflect for a moment, you will see that it is the heretics rather than the orthodox who are, of all men, the most given to preaching. Bishops preach as a matter of duty; Savonarola and Mr Shaw preach for the religious pleasure of it. So rare a thing is it to find an orthodox clergyman of standing doing anything that deserves the name of preaching—and by preaching I mean protesting in capable words against the subordination of life to luxury—that, whenever he does so, the newspapers put it on their posters among the great events, like a scandal about a Cabinet Minister or an earthquake.

It is not difficult to see why the preachers have usually been so doubtful about the dancers. It is simply that dancing is for the most part a rhythmical pantomime of sex. It is the most haremish of pastimes. One is not surprised to learn that Henry VIII was the most expert of royal dancers. He was an enthusiast for the kissing dances of his day, indeed, even before he had abandoned his youthful straitness for the moral code of a farmyard that had gone off its head. I can imagine how a preacher with his craft at his fingers' ends could deduce Henry's downfall from those first delicate trippings. Even the *Encyclopædia Britannica* is driven to admit the presence of the amorous element in dancing. "Actual contact of the partners," it insists, "is quite intelligible as matter of pure dancing; for, apart altogether from the pleasure of the embrace, the harmony of the double rotation adds very much to the enjoyment." But that reference to "the pleasure of the embrace" is fatal to the sentence. How are we simple people as we whirl in the waltz to know whether it is the pleasure of the embrace or the harmony of the double rotation that is making us glow so? The preachers will certainly not give us the benefit of the doubt. They will follow the lead of Byron, who, in his horror at the popularisation of the waltz, declared that Terpsichore was henceforth "the least a vestal virgin of the Nine." Many people will remember the letter which Byron prefaced to *The Waltz* over the signature of Horace Hornem, supposed to be a country gentleman from the Midlands. Describing his sensations on first seeing his wife waltzing, Mr Hornem says:—

> Judge of my surprise ... to see poor Mrs Hornem with her arms half round the loins of a huge hussar-looking gentleman I never set eyes on before; and his, to say truth, rather more than half round her waist, turning round, and round, and round, to a d——d see-saw, up-and-down sort of tune, that reminded me of the "Black joke."

Cynics explain Byron's attitude to dancing as a matter of envy, since he himself was too lame to waltz. At the same time, I fancy that an anthropologist from Mars, if he visited the earth, would take the same view of the drama of the waltz as Byron did. I do not mean to say that the waltz cannot be danced in a sublime innocence. It can, and often is. But the point is that sex is the arch-musician of it, and whether you approve of waltzing or disapprove of it will depend upon whether, like the preachers, you regard sex as Aholah and Aholibah, or, like the poets, as April and the song of the stars. It is worth remembering in this connection that a great preacher like Huxley took much the same view of poetry that Byron took of dancing. Most of it, he said, seemed to him to be little more than sensual caterwauling. Tolstoi, if I am not mistaken, interpreted *Romeo and Juliet* in the same spirit. This kind of analysis, whether it is just or foolish, always shocks the crowd, which can never admit the existence of the senses without blushing for them. Confirmed in its sentimentalism—and therefore given to "harping on the sensual string"—it swears that it finds the Russian ballet more edifying than church, and would have no objection to seeing the Merry Widow waltz introduced into a mothers' meeting. There is nothing in which we are such hypocrites as our pleasures. That is why some of us like the preachers. Even if they are grossly inhuman in wanting to take our amusements away from us, they at least insist that we shall submit them to a realistic analysis. In this they are excellent servants of the scientific spirit.

What, then, is a reasonable attitude to adopt towards sex in dancing? Obviously we cannot abolish sex, even if we wished to do so. And if we try to chain it up, it will merely become crabbed like a dog. On the other hand, there is all the difference in the world between putting a dog on a chain and encouraging it to go mad and bite half the parish. There is nearly as wide a distance separating the courtly dances of the eighteenth century from the cake-walk, and the apache dance from the Irish reel. Priests, I know, in whom the gift of preaching has turned sour, have been as severe on innocent as on furious dances. But this is merely an exaggeration of the prevailing sense of mankind that sex is a wild animal and most difficult to tame into a fireside pet. It is upon the civilisation of this animal, none the less, though not upon the butchering of it, that the decencies of the world depend. And this is exercise for a hero, for the animal in question has a desperate tendency to revert to type. One noticed how its eye bulged with the memory of African forests when the cake-walk affronted the sun a few years ago. The cake-walk, I admit, seemed a right and rapturous thing enough when it was danced by those in whose veins was the recent blood of Africa. But when young gentlemen began to introduce it as a figure in the lancers in suburban back-parlours one resented it, not merely as an emasculated parody, but as an act of dishonest innocence. But everywhere it has been the tendency of dancing in recent years to become more noisily sexual. I am not thinking of the dancing in undress which for a time captured the music-halls. That is almost the least sexual dancing we have had. The dancing of Isidora Duncan was of as good report as a painting by old Sir Joshua. We may pass over the Russian ballet, too, because of the art which often raised it to beauty, though it is interesting to speculate what St Bernard would have thought of Nijinsky. But, as for rag-time, it is a silly madness, a business for Mænads of both sexes; and all those gesticulations of the human frame known as bunny-hugs, turkey-trots, and the rest of it are condemned by their very names as tolerable only in the menagerie. On the other hand, because the bunny in man and the turkey in woman have revived themselves with such impudence, are we to get out our guns against all dancing? Far from it. One is not going to sacrifice the flowery grace of Genée, or Pavlova with her genius of the butterflies, because of the multitude of fools. All we can do is to insist upon the recognition of the fact that dancing may be good or bad, as eggs are good or bad, and to remind the world that in dancing, as in eggs, freshness is even more beautiful than decadence. Perhaps some of the performances of the Russian ballet would come off limping from such a test. Opinions will differ about that. In any case, one cannot help the logic of one's belief. Each of us, no doubt, contains something of the preacher and something of the dancer; and our enthusiasms depend upon which of the two is dominant in us. Meanwhile, we are likely to go on preaching against our dancing, and dancing against our preaching, till the end of time. That merely proves the completeness of our humanity. It makes for balance, like, as I have said, east and west in a map. That, surely, is a conclusion which ought to satisfy everybody.

IV
THOUGHTS AT A TANGO TEA

It is not easy to decide what is the dullest feature in the Tango Teas upon which Londoners are now wasting their afternoons and their silver. The most disconcertingly tedious part of the whole entertainment is, in my opinion, the Tango itself: it is mere virtuoso-work in dancing—an eccentric caper, not after beauty, but after variety. But the rest of the programme has no compensating liveliness. The songs are sad affairs, even for a music-hall, and the band, with its continual "selections" dropped into every available hole in the afternoon's amusement, gets on the nerves like a tune played over and over again. And then, to crown everything, comes the parade of mannequins wearing the latest fashions in women's dress, or what will be the latest fashions in another month or two. On the whole I think this part of the show must be given the prize for inanity. The Tango is bad, and the tea varies, but this milliner's business—it is more than dull, it is an outrage on human intelligence.

Students of society cannot afford to leave unnoticed this new development in the tastes of the upper and middle classes. It seems to me to represent almost the extreme limit in the evolution of the English theatre. The actor-managers have often in recent years turned Shakespeare into a dress parade, but here is the dress parade with Shakespeare left out. Musical comedies, hundreds of them, have been as amazing as fireworks with their wonder of costumes, and here is the wonder of costumes without any alloy of musical comedy. Nor are these costumes flashed upon you with a chorussed insolence. Slowly and separately each girl appears, sometimes from the back of the stalls, sometimes from the back of the stage, and marches before your vision as obtrusive as an advertisement, while the band plays some tune like "You made me love you." One should not say "marches" perhaps, but glides. The glide seems to be the ideal at which the modern woman aims in her walk, and the mannequin glides with every exaggeration. But, if you have ever seen cows ambling along a country road you have seen something strangely like the glide that is now in fashion, yet no one thinks of speaking of cows as "gliding." The mannequins come before us one by one at this slow cattle-walk, and pass along one of those Reinhardt pathways above the heads of the people in the stalls. Then they raise their arms and turn round as in a showroom and smile as in the advertisement of a tooth-wash. And so on till ten or a dozen of them have appeared and disappeared. Then out glides the whole school of them again not singly this time, but in a procession, all smiling under their barbaric panaches and their towering crest of feathers, and one of them with her head and chin wrapped in gilt embroideries that make her look like a queen with a toothache. All smiles and paint, the girls nevertheless seem to have no more relation to their gowns than a statue to the hat which someone has perched on its head. They give us no drama of dress. They are simply lay-figures imitating the colours of the rainbow. Perhaps, to a student of fashion, they have some meaning and interest. But a student of fashion does not go for his lessons to a music-hall. To the rest of us they are simply a trash of fine clothes. They are a decadent substitute for gladiatorial exhibitions. They are a last wild—no, no; not wild—a last tame parody on life. Life as a parade of mannequins—the satiric imagination could invent nothing more contemptuously comic. Perhaps, in the theatre of the future, the characters of the plays will remain as mannequins, while the words will be left out as superfluous. Hamlet will appear in his inky cloak at the right intervals, turn round so as to give us a good back and front view, and Ophelia will then take his place in a procession of fine dresses, the whole play being a solemn in-and-out movement of silent gowned figures. Shakespeare ought to be much more popular that way. Even Shakespeare on the cinematograph could hardly compete with it.

What, one wonders, is the cause of all this mannequinism? Is it a survival of the passion for dolls? Or is it a case of woman's flying to a refuge after man has ousted her from all her old busy pleasures? Scarcely anything but the dress interest is left to her. Woman—at least the kind of woman whom one sees at Tango Teas—no longer bakes, or weaves, or spins, or makes medicines, or even sews as her grandmothers—or, to be quite accurate, her grandmothers' grandmothers—did. She has gradually been led to hand over her baking to the baker, her medicines to the chemist, her weaving and spinning to the mills. What could Penelope herself do in such circumstances? Without her loom there would have been nothing for her but to think out fresh ways of arranging her hair and to disguise herself endlessly in new draperies which would have led to her being pestered more than ever by the suitors. Idleness, it does not take a Sunday-school teacher to see, is the universal dressmaker, and a woman who is not allowed to work and does not drink and has not even a vote is driven among the mannequins as surely as if you forced her there by law. After all, if one has nothing to do, one must do something. One must put one's virtue into hats and stockings if one is not allowed to practise it more soberly. It may be, of course, that the mannequin stage which the women of the comfortable classes have now reached is really a step towards a more sober dignity. Woman had to be released from the old servitude of the house—from the predestined making of beds and sewing of clothes and cooking of dinners—in order to assert her equal capacities with those of the man who rode to war and cozened his fellows in the city and sat on committees and stayed out till all hours. She may not have realised at the time that it was merely an escape from one drudgery to another—from the drudgery of housework to the drudgery of pleasure—but she cannot take her brains with her into a music-hall matinée without realising it now. And she is learning to hate the one as much as the other. Feminism is woman's great protest against the drudgery of pleasure. Some of the feminists, it may be granted, turn it into a claim to share with man all those old pleasures with which man's eyes have long been yellow and weary. But the spectacle of the middle-aged male followers of the life of pleasure in any restaurant or theatre ought to terrify these bold ladies from maintaining such a demand. The supreme philosophers of pleasure, from Epicurus to Stevenson, have all had to turn to hard work and virtue as the only forms of amusement which did not spoil the bloom of one's cheek. Even the supreme philosopher of clothes would have kept us far too busy ever to think about them.

People unfortunately have got it into their heads, as the result of a long process of civilisation, that, in order to be beautiful, clothes must be a kind of finery to which one gives the thoughts of one's nights and days. And the result is that most women would rather take the advice of their dressmaker than of Epicurus. It is one of the most ludicrous misdirections that the human race has ever followed. The dressmaker's living depends on her keeping off Epicurus with one hand and the Twelve Apostles with the other, and she has certainly done so with the most brilliant efficiency. We who do not live by dressmaking, however, should be coolly critical of the dressmaker's point of view. It was not she, perhaps, who invented, but it is she who most brazenly keeps alive, the great delusion of civilised society that woman's foolish dresses are more beautiful than the reasonable clothes of men. In fifteen thousand years or so, when the idea of beauty will have had time to develop into a tiny bud, men and supermen will laugh at this old absurdity. The idea that modern men's clothes are ugly is a deception chiefly maintained by advertisement agents and shopkeepers. There is, I admit, much to be said against the bowler hat. But the jacket, the trousers, and the sock—so long as it does not match the tie—come nearer what is excellent and appropriate in dress than any other costume that has been invented since the strong silent Englishman left his coat of paint behind him in the wood. It is possible, no doubt, to spoil the effect of it all with too much folding and pressing. Dandyism means the ruin of one's clothes from the æsthetic point of view. One must be ready to expose them to all weathers—to have them rained upon and rumpled—if one wants them to be really beautiful, say, like an old church.

It is because woman's dress at its finest does not stand this test of beauty that a marchioness is worse clad than the driver of a coal cart or a chimney-sweep. Not luxury, but necessity, is the creator of beauty. Beauty comes from our submission to Nature; it is not a matter of thieving a few handfuls of coloured feathers from Nature's breast and wings. It comes by accident, as you will see if you look down from a hill at night on a gas-lit town. Almost the only kind of lights which are not beautiful are those which are deliberately so. One has to go out of the streets among the lights of the White City in order to see beauty giving way to prettiness. Similarly, one might say that the only kind of dresses which are not beautiful are those which are deliberately so. Even among the poor there is more grace to be found among mill-girls in their shawls than when on Sundays they dress themselves up to look as like their dream of riches as possible. I hope that the dress parades in the West End theatres and music-halls will sooner or later be transferred to the poorer districts. They may not at once kill envy and the respect for wealth. They may not strike people as being so ridiculous as they really are, though anyone who finds amusement in waxworks ought to get sufficient entertainment from a dress parade. But if the show has not this effect, it may at least open the eyes of the poor to the barbarous conditions in which the rich live and fire them with the determination to hurry to the rescue and release them from the gilded cage of their luxuries. The beginning of the social revolution, I foresee, will be a rising against the mannequins. It will be an infinitely greater event in history than the taking of the Bastille.

V
THE HUMOURS OF MURDER

Almost everyone who has committed a murder knows that the business has its tragic side. Whether it also has its comic side is a question that has been raised since the production of Sir James Barrie's play, *The Adored One*. This, as most people are aware, is a farce about a lady who kills a man by pushing him out of a railway carriage because he will not allow the window to be shut. Some of the critics have protested that the theme is too grim for light entertainment. They are, most of them, probably, lovers of fresh air, who foresee a new danger in railway travel if women—creatures already enjoying the possession of an extremely feeble moral sense—are taught to regard the murder of a hygienic fellow-passenger as a laughing matter. Some years ago, when *The Playboy of the Western World* was first put on the stage in Dublin, there were similar denunciations of the idea of making a comedy of murder. It was then considered, however, that nobody outside Ireland could take murder so seriously as to miss seeing the joke of it. As a matter of fact, I believe the average respectable man all the world over would side in his heart with the Dublin demonstrators. Murder is, after all, one of the oldest institutions on earth. It dates from the second generation of the human race. It is almost as venerable as a sin can be, and to treat it flippantly is as shocking to comfortable ears as the blasphemies of a boy. Everybody knows how Baudelaire used to shock the citizens of Brussels by opening his conversation in cafés in a raised voice with the words: "The night I killed my father." He has himself related how he began the thing as a joke in order to punish the Belgians for believing everything he said. "Exasperated by always being believed," he wrote, "I spread the report that I had killed my father, and that I had eaten him, and that if I had been allowed to escape from France it was only on account of the services I had rendered to the French police, and I was BELIEVED!"

That is the penalty of the jester on serious subjects like murder. He is nearly always believed. The very mention of prepense death puts a great many people into a solemn mood that is hostile to wit and humour and any kind of facetiousness. I have met men and women, for instance, who were quite unable to see the entertaining side of cannibalism. Gilbert's ballad of the *Nancy Lee*, about the cook who gradually ate all the rest of the crew, moves them not to laughter but to horror. When the cook, or somebody else, as he gobbles one of his mates, enthusiastically exclaims: "Oh, how like pig!" they merely shudder. Those of us who are amused, on the other hand, are so only because we are not such inveterate realists as our neighbours. We treat comic murders as Charles Lamb treated comic cuckoldries. We regard them as happening, not in our world of realities, but in a kind of no-man's-land of humour. If it were not so, we should probably be as shocked as anyone else — those of us, that is, who are old-fashioned enough to consider murder and adultery as on the whole reprehensible. Luckily, human beings in the mass have gradually developed an artistic sense which enables them to leave the world of serious facts for the world of comic pretences at a moment's notice. And even the strictest humanitarian can smile with a good conscience at the most hideous of the tortures—"something with boiling oil in it"—discussed in the paper-fan world of *The Mikado*. I can imagine a sensitive child's being sharply disturbed by the punishments that at one time seem to be in store for so many of the characters in the opera. But for the rest of us Gilbert's Japan is as unreal as a nest of insects, where even the crimes seem funny. In the same way we have made a child's joke of Bluebeard, whose prototype was at least as atrocious a character as Jack the Ripper. Perhaps, in some distant island of the South Seas, where Europe is sufficiently remote to be unreal, the children are already enjoying the humours of Jack the Ripper in the local substitute for the Christmas pantomime.

Even a real murder, however, may strike one as amusing, if only it has about it something incongruous. A thousand people have laughed for one who has wept over Wainwright's murder of Helen Abercrombie, not because it was not a filthy deed, but because the murderer, on being reproached for it, uttered his famous reply: "Yes; it was a dreadful thing to do, but she had very thick ankles." Here it is the incongruity between the deed and the excuse for it that appeals to our sense of humour. We laugh at it as we would laugh at Milton's Satan if we saw him dressed in baby clothes. Similarly, when Peer Gynt and the Cook fight after the shipwreck for possession of the place of safety on the upturned boat, and Peer in effect murders the Cook, the situation is comic because of the incongruity between what is said and what is done. Take, for instance, the Lord's Prayer scene:

> The Cook (*slipping*): I'm drowning!
>
> Peer (*seizing him*): By this wisp of hair
> I'll hold you; say your Lord's Prayer, quick!
>
> The Cook: I can't remember; all turns black— —
>
> Peer: Come, the essentials in a word!
>
> The Cook: Give us this day— —!

Peer: Skip that part, Cook.
You'll get all *you* need, safe enough.

The Cook: Give us this day — —

Peer: The same old song!
'Tis plain you were a cook in life — —

    (The Cook *slips from his grasp*.)

The Cook (*sinking*): Give us this day our — —
(*Disappears.*)

Peer: Amen, lad!
To the last gasp you were yourself.
(*Draws himself up on to the bottom of the boat.*)
So long as there is life there's hope.

It is the paradox that delights us here — the exquisite inappropriateness of Peer's invitation to the Cook to say a prayer before he lets him dip under for the last time, and of the only petition which the Cook can remember in his extremity. The latter amuses us like Mr George Moore's story about the Irish poet who was asked to say a prayer when out in a curragh on Galway Bay during a furious gale, and who astonished the boat's crew by beginning: "Of man's first disobedience and the fruit." Even in *The Playboy* it is the humours of the inappropriate that make Christy Mahon's narrative of how he slew his da comic. One remembers the sentence in which he first lets the secret of his deed slip out:

> Christy: Don't strike me. I killed my poor father, Tuesday was a week, for doing the like of that.
>
> Pegeen (*in blank amazement*): Is it killed your father?
>
> Christy (*subsiding*): With the help of God I did surely, and that the Holy Immaculate Mother may intercede for his soul.

There you have incongruity to a point that shocks an ordinary Christian like a blasphemy. And Christy's reflection, as he finds that the supposed murder has made him a hero — "I'm thinking this night wasn't I a foolish fellow not to kill my father in the years gone by" — tickles us because it brings a new and incongruous standard to the measurement of moral values. De Quincey's essay, "On Murder considered as one of the Fine Arts," owes its reputation for humour to the same kind of unexpectedness in its table of values. At least, that passage in which the lecturer of the essay describes the warning he gave to a new servant whom he suspected of dabbling in murder plays a delightful topsy-turvy game with our everyday moral world:

> If once a man indulges himself in murder, very soon he comes to think very little of robbing; and from robbing he

comes next to drinking and Sabbath breaking, and from
that to incivility and procrastination. Once begin upon this
downward path, you never know where you are to stop.
Many a man has dated his ruin from some murder or other
that perhaps he thought little of at the time.

Humour is largely a matter of new proportions and unexpected
elements. And it visits the gaol as readily as the music-hall, and attends us
in our hearse no less than in our perambulator. Self-murder is not in itself a
funny subject, but who can remain solemn over the case of the man who put
an end to his life because he got tired of all the buttoning and unbuttoning.
Similarly, detestable a crime as we may think cannibalism, we cannot help
smiling when a traveller notes, as a recent traveller in West Africa did, that
human flesh never gives the eater indigestion as the flesh of beasts does.
It is—at least, I suppose it is—merely a statement of fact, but it amuses us
because it introduces an inappropriate and unexpected element into our
consideration of cannibalism.

Perhaps Sir James Barrie would prefer to defend the humour of *The
Adored One* on the ground, not that it is the humour of unreality, but that,
like the examples I have quoted, it is the humour of incongruity. And,
indeed, we only laugh at Leonora's murder in the train because the reason
for it was so disproportionate to the crime. It is not funny for a woman to kill
a man because he has beaten her black and blue. It is not funny for her to kill
him for his money, or for any other reasonable motive. On the other hand,
it would be funny if she killed him for smoking a pipe while wearing a tall
hat, or because he said "lay" instead of "lie." It is the unreason of the thing
that appeals to us, and no amount of theorising about the immorality of
murder can deprive us of our joke. At the same time one is willing to admit
the excellence of those people who are so overwhelmed by the exceeding
sinfulness of sin that they cannot raise a smile over even the most ridiculous
scenes of murder and marital infidelity. I know a great many people who
can see nothing comic in the upside-down antics of the drunken; they feel
as if in laughing at the absurdities of vice they would be acquiescing in vice.
Perhaps they would. Perhaps laughter is given to sinners as a compensation
for sins. It makes us tolerant by making us cheerful, and if we could
really laugh at murders and all indecencies, we should possibly end in
thinking that they are far less black than they are painted. So, I imagine, the
unlaughing saints reason. They always visualise sin in its horror in a way
that is beyond most of us, and we can respect their gloom. But we who are
more complex than the saints—we know well enough that so paradoxical

an affair is the human soul that a man may laugh and laugh and keep the Ten Commandments; and we claim the right, on the plea that "my mind to me a kingdom is," of maintaining a court fool in our hearts to parody our royal existence, and so keep it from going stale. In any case, we can no more help laughing than we can help the colour of our hair. That is why we shall go on laughing at the humours of the seven deadly sins, and why old scoundrels like Nero and Gilles de Retz and Henry VIII are likely to remain favourite characters in the comic chapters of human life till the book is burnt and a new volume opens.

VI
THE DECLINE AND FALL OF HELL

It is significant of the change that has come over the religious imagination that a number of representative clergymen have issued a manifesto of disbelief in Hell and no heresy-hunt has begun. Disbelief in Hell, it must in fairness be added, not as a symbol of something sufficiently real, but as a definite place on the map of the Universe, a gulf of wild flame and red-hot torments without end. There was a time when to doubt any jot or tittle in the scenery and rhetoric of Hell would have been thought a kind of atheism, and a world without Hell would have seemed to many religious minds almost as lonely as a world without God. Life was conceived chiefly in terms of Hell. It was a kind of tight-rope walk across a bottomless pit of shooting fires and the intolerable wailing of the damned. Heaven was sought less almost for its proper delights than as an escape from the malignance of the demons in this vast torture-chamber. Hell, indeed, was the most desperately real of countries. For centuries men studied its geography with greater zeal of research than we devote to-day to the geography of Africa. They described its rule and estimated its population, one author, with how much belief I know not, detailing the names of seventy-two of its princes with 7,405,926 devils serving them. In *The Apocalypse of St Peter*, which is as old at least as the second century, the occupations of the damned are set forth with a horrid carefulness. Hell is depicted as a continent of lakes of fire and burning mud, over which adulterers hang by the hair and blasphemers of the way of righteousness by the tongue. False witnesses chew tongues of fire in their mouths. Misers roll on red-hot stones sharper than spikes. Men who have committed unnatural crimes are endlessly hurled from the top of dreadful crags. And this is but one of the first of a long line of visions of the hereafter which appeared, like the season's fruits, all through the early Christian centuries and the Middle Ages, and achieved their perfect statement in Dante. Every new writer sought out the most exquisite torments a sensational imagination could invent, and added them to the picture of the daily life of Hell and Purgatory. The Monk of Evesham saw in his dream of Purgatory men being fried in a pan and others "pierced with fiery nails even to their bones and to the loosening of their joints." Others were gnawed by worms or dragged with hooks, or hung on gallows, or "soaked in baths of pitch and brimstone with a horrible stench," and, if they tried to escape, "the devils that met with them beat them sorely with scourges and forks and other kinds of torments." But we need not go back beyond our own days for instances of these torturing imaginations. Many who are now living have had the night-fears of their childhood made monstrous with stories of devils with red-hot pincers to tear one's flesh and with red-hot nails to lacerate one's back. I have a friend who loves to tell of the regular Sunday summons of an ancient clergyman to his congregation to flee from the doom of the condemned sinner whom he invariably pictured as "seated upon a projecting crag over a lurid, hissing, moaning, raging sea of an undone Eternity, calling out, 'The harvest is past and I am not savèd.'"

Why the human imagination did not revolt against such a painful orgy of sensationalism long before it did, it is difficult to understand. Lecky tells us that the only prominent theologian to dispute the material fire of Hell throughout the Middle Ages was the Irishman Johannes Scotus Erigena. All the others accepted it either in terror or with delight. For who can question that men can obtain as fiercely sensual a pleasure from inflicting the pains of Hell on their enemies as from flogging children and slaves? One of the best known instances of this—shall I say, hellish?—sensualism, is the appeal of Tertullian to his fellow Christians not to attend public spectacles on the ground that they would one day behold the far more glorious spectacle of the heathen rolling in the flames of the Pit.

> "What," he wrote, "shall be the magnitude of that scene? How shall I wonder? How shall I laugh? How shall I rejoice? How shall I triumph when I behold so many and such illustrious kings, who were said to be mounted into heaven groaning with Jupiter their god in the lowest darkness of Hell! Then shall the soldiers who persecuted the name of Christ burn in more cruel fire than any they had kindled for the saints.... Compared with such spectacles, with such subjects of triumph as these, what can praetor or consul, quaestor or pontiff, afford? And even now faith can bring them near, imagination can depict them as present."

Thus, Hell became the poor man's consolation, the oppressed and baited man's revenge. Sleep itself hardly brought greater balm that the thought of this large engulfing doom for opprobrious neighbours. It would be unfair, on the other hand, to suggest that the ordinary Christian ever believed in Hell save in honest misery of heart. "O, Lord," an old lay evangelist used to pray in the homes he visited, "shake these Thy children over Hell-fire, but shake them in marcy!" There you have the voice of one who regarded Hell, not with glee as the end of his enemies, but with desperate earnestness as a necessary moral agency—who believed that men must be terrorised into virtue or never know virtue at all. And, it is interesting to note, a clerical correspondent has been writing to the *Daily News* expressing the same gloomy view. This writer declares, as the fruit of long experience, that he has never known a case of a man's being converted except through fear. It is common enough, too—or used to be—to hear church-going young men profess that if they did not believe in Hell, they would amaze the earth with their lusts and exploits. Viewed in this light, the Devil becomes the world's super-policeman, and those who seek to abolish him will naturally be looked on as dangerous anarchists who would destroy the foundations of the law. As for that, it would be foolish to deny the great part played by fear in the lives both of sinners and saints, but whether morality is ultimately served by our being afraid of the wrong things is a question that calls for consideration. Certainly, Hell has produced its crop of devils as well as of saints upon earth. It was men who believed in Hell who invented the thumb-screw and the rack, and many of the most fiendish instruments of torture the world has known.

Whether it is the case that man made Hell because he believed in torture, or took to torture because he believed in Hell, there is no denying that the worst period of torture our European civilisation has known coincided with the time when men believed that God Himself doomed to savage and eternal torments men, women, and even infants in the cradle, on the most paltry excuses. And as man's conscience has more and more decisively forbidden him to use torture as a punishment, it has also forbidden him to believe that a beneficent Deity could do such a thing. It may be thought that a beneficent Deity who could permit cancer and the Putumayo and the factory system at its worst, might easily enough sanction the fires of the mediæval Hell. But even cancer and the Putumayo are not a denial of what Stevenson called "the ultimate decency of things." They are temporary, not eternal. Thoughtful Christians can no longer accept the old Hell, because it would mean, not the final triumph of righteousness, but the final defeat of God. Many of those who dutifully cling to the dogma of their Church on the point would agree with the French curé who said that he believed in Hell, but he did not think there was anybody in it except Voltaire. And even Voltaire will nowadays seem to most people to be hardly a sufficiently scandalous person to deserve infinite millions of years of anguish. The truth is, Hell shocks our moral sense. Tennyson put the modern disbelief in it with a theatrical forcibleness when he said that, if after death he woke up, even though it should be in Heaven, and found there was a Hell, he would turn round and shake his fist in the face of God Almighty. Since Tennyson's time Hell's foundations have subsided: the ancient flames have died down; and man has now for the background of his days no fierce and devouring universe, but a cricket score-board and a page of "thinklet" competitions in a penny paper. Perhaps the antithesis is an unfair one, but some cosmic sense has certainly been lost to the general imagination. No doubt it will return as moral ideas take the place of materialistic terrors; for out of the wreck of the fiery Hell a moral Hell is already rising. A moral Purgatory, one ought to say—a place of discipline made in the image of this disciplining earth. For the terrors of death and evil and pain all survive, and, even if we abolish utterly the Devil with the pitchfork, and put in his place the Button-moulder, is that a figure a pennyworth less dreadful? No, the escape from Hell is not so much a holiday as we thought. There is still an interval of adventure between us and Paradise, and all the perils and fears to be overcome as of old. We have chased an allegory from our doors, but its ghostly reality returns and stands outside the window. And salvation and damnation remain the two chief facts under the sun. And the saints and the parsons—and everybody, indeed, except gloating old Tertullian—were right after all.

VII
ON CHEERFUL READERS

There has been an increasing demand lately for cheerful books. Mr Balfour began it—at least, he gave it a voice by quoting approvingly a phrase from one of Mr Bennett's novels about the books that cheer us all up. It was a most unfortunate phrase to quote in public. It confirmed every bald old scaramouch in all his hostilities to realism, tragedy, and every other form of literature that does not go about with its hat over its eye. It also confirmed a popular prejudice to the effect that it is the duty of men of letters to be cheerful in a way in which it is not the duty, say, of mathematicians to be cheerful. Now, one need not be an enemy of cheerfulness to detest this theory. One merely needs to be sufficiently awake to recognise that cheerfulness may easily become a tyranny which will bind the hands and feet of literature as it has already bound the hands and feet of drama. Cheerfulness, cheerfulness, and yet again cheerfulness, is the all too golden rule in the theatre. One result of this is that Ibsen has been expelled from the stage for the only naughtiness of which the English theatre takes notice—the naughtiness of being serious. Even Mr Shaw, who possesses the comic spirit in greater abundance than any other writer of his time, is flayed alive by the critics on the production of each new play he writes, because, besides being cheerful, he is a man of ideas. It is not enough that you should be cheerful: you must be cheerful to the exclusion of everything else—everything, at least, that might bring unrest to the intellect or the spirit or to any other part of a man except the muscles that work the oil-wells of sentiment and the creaking jaws of laughter. The consequences might have been foreseen. No one unaided, could be quite so inhumanly vacuous as the audiences in the theatres expected him to be. And so the dramatic author had to call in to his aid the musicians, the poets, the limelight-men, the mask-sellers, the dancing girls, the dressmakers, and a host of other people, each of whom separately could only be a little inane, but all of whom together could be overwhelmingly inane; and among them they produced that overwhelming inanity, musical comedy. There you have the ultimate logic of cheerfulness in the theatre. It is like the obtrusive cheerfulness of the performing animals in music-halls. It is a tedious and beastly thing. It is cheerfulness without mind or meaning. It is like a laugh painted on a clown's face. Compulsory cheerfulness must always end like that, because, if one has to laugh all the time, it is far easier to put the laugh on with a brush than to keep one's face distorted by strength of will.

With the warning of the cheerful theatre before us, then, it would be the stupidest folly to pay any heed to the new plea for cheerful books. It is an extraordinary fact that thousands of people can be serious to the point of bad temper over a political argument or a game of cards or tennis; but if you asked them to take a book seriously, they would regard the prospect as worse than a dry pharyngitis. They put literature on a level not with their games, but with the chocolates and drinks they consume when they are resting from their games. It is of the chocolate kind of literature that ninety-nine out of a hundred persons are thinking when they applaud phrases about the books that cheer us all up. Or it might be nearer the mark to liken the sort of literature they have in mind to one of those brands of medicated port which innocent old ladies find grateful and comforting. We live in an age of advertised brain-fag, and we demand of literature that it shall be the literature of brain-fag. We ask of it not friendship, but a drug. That is the heresy which must be killed if letters are to live. Till it is killed they will not even be enjoyed. I grant at once that it would be an impudence to expect an average sensual man to regard books with the same profound interest as his business affairs or his wife. On the other hand, persuade him that it is pleasant to put as much of his heart into the enjoyment of a book as he puts into the enjoyment of a football match, and you will produce a revolution among the book-reading public. No man who is not eccentric dreams of asking that a football match shall be amusing or a game of chess cheerful. He goes to the one for its furious energy, for the thrill of the rivalry of real people; he turns to the other for an experience of intensity, of prescient skill. It is for energetic experiences of a comparable kind, as Mr R. A. Scott-James suggestively pointed out in a recent volume, that we go to literature. Literature is not primarily meant to cheer us up when we are too tired to read the paper, though incidentally it often does so, and to despise this kind of literature would be as sinful as to despise Christmas pudding and brandy sauce. But the purpose of literature is not to be an epilogue to energy. It involves not a slackening, but a change, of effort. That is why even the difficult authors like the Browning of *Sordello* attract us. They have the appeal of pathless mountains. It is a curious fact, at the same time, that some of those who delight most boldly in physical experiences turn from intellectual and imaginative experiences with a kind of contempt. They despise from their hearts the mollycoddle who will not risk a wound or a cold for the pleasures of the sun and air. But, so far as the imagination is concerned, they themselves are mollycoddles who will not venture beyond a game of halma or a sugarstick by the hearth. What the world of literature needs most is not cheerful writers, but adventurous readers. The reading of poetry will become as popular as swimming when once it is recognised that it is as natural and as exhilarating.

Literature thus justifies itself not so much by cheering us all up when we are limp as by its appeal to the spirit of adventure, or, if you like the phrase better, the spirit of experience. That is the explanation of the pleasure we take in tragic literature. Tragedy reminds certain spiritual energies in us that they are alive. It enables them to expand, to exert themselves, to breathe freely. That is why, in literature, it makes us happy to be miserable. To put forth our strength, whether of limb or of imagination, makes for our happiness far more than the passive cheerfulness of the fireside; or if not more, at least as much. It would be ungrateful to speak slightingly of the easy-chair and its pleasures. But the chief danger in literature at present is not that the easy-chair will be neglected, but that it will be given a place of far too great importance. Hence it is necessary to emphasise the pleasures of the strenuous life in contrast. This may seem to some readers a tolerable excuse for liking tragedy and poetry, but a poor defence of the taste for realism, naturalism, or whatever you like to call it. Even those who respond immediately to the appeal of the mountains and the sea will often resist the invitation of Zola and Huysmans and their followers to seek adventures in the slums. They will not see that it is as natural to go on one's travels in the slums as in the most beautiful lakeland on earth. As a matter of fact, the discovery of the slums was one of the most tremendous discoveries of the nineteenth century. It was one of those revolutionary discoveries that have changed our whole view of society. Whether it was the men of letters or the sociologists who first discovered them I do not know. I contend, however, that the men of letters had as much right to go to them as the sociologists. They found life expressed there in horror and beauty, in sordidness and nobility, and to reveal this in literature was to some extent to create a new world for the imagination. It was to do more than this. Society could not become fully self-conscious or articulate until the pauper aspect of it was expressed in literature. Hence the novelist of mean streets extended the boundaries of social self-consciousness. The realists indeed have brought the remedial imagination to us as the sociologist has brought the remedial facts and figures. This remedialism, no doubt, is an extra-literary interest. But nothing is quite alien to literature which touches the imagination. The imagination may find its treasures in Tyre and Sidon or in an alley off a back street, or even in a semi-detached villa. One must not limit it in its wanderings to safe and clean and comfortable places.

This seems to me to be the great justification of the demand, not for cheerful books, but for cheerful and courageous readers. The cheerful reader will be able to go to hell with Dante and to hospital with Esther Waters; and though this may be but a poor and secondhand courage, it is at least preferable to the intellectual and imaginative cowardice which will admit danger into literature only when it has been stripped of every semblance of reality. The courage of the study, it may be, is not so fine a thing as the courage of the workshop and the field. But it is finer than is generally admitted. And it is much rarer. There is no place in which men and women are so shamelessly lazy and timid as among their books. If happiness lay in that direction, the laziness might be justified. But it does not. Happiness can never come from the atrophy of nine-tenths of our nature. It is the result of the vigorous delight of heart and mind and spirit as well as of body. The cheerful reader feels as ready for Æschylus and his furies as the yachtsman for his sail on a choppy sea. He fears the tragic satire of *Madame Bovary* no more than a good pedestrian fears the east wind. This is not to say that he does not enjoy cheerful books when he finds them. He may even prefer *Tristram Shandy* and *The Pickwick Papers* to Tolstoi. But he realises that cheerfulness in a book is a delightful accident, not a necessity of literature. He knows that to be cheerful is his own business, whether he goes with his author into the dark and solitary places or into the sheltered and smiling gardens of the sun.

VIII
ST G. B. S. AND THE BISHOP

There has been a delightful correspondence going on in the *Times* about Mdlle Gaby Deslys. It owed not a little of its charm, I suspect, to the fact that none of the correspondents had seen Gaby. The Bishop of Kensington had not seen her; Mr H. B. Irving had not seen her; Mr Bernard Shaw had not seen her. So they quarrelled furiously over her as men have always quarrelled over the unseen, and if Æsop had been alive, he might have got a fable out of the affair. The Bishop made the mistake at the beginning of calling upon the Censor to suppress Gaby. Mr Shaw, at mention of the Censor, immediately saw red, and Gaby of the Lilies presented herself to his inflamed vision as a beautiful damsel who was about to be made a meal of by an ecclesiastical monster. He at once challenged the Bishop to battle—a battle of theories. The Bishop unfortunately had no theory with him. He took his stand upon the law. After the manner of Shylock, he insisted upon his pound of flesh. Mr Shaw, of course, who bristled with theories could not stand this. So he gave the Bishop his choice of theories and even put several into his mouth, and forced a conflict upon him. And it was a famous victory.

> But what they fought each other for
> I could not well make out.

Perhaps Mr Shaw himself did not quite know. But he made during the fight some weird statements which are well worth examination.

One of these was that, in regard to sex as in regard to religion, it is very difficult to say what is good and what is evil, and more difficult still to suppress the one without suppressing the other. So much is this so according to Mr Shaw that "one man seeing a beautiful actress will feel that she has made all common debaucheries impossible to him; another seeing the same actress in the same part will plunge straight into those debaucheries because he has seen her body without seeing her soul." But why choose a beautiful actress for the argument? This matter can only be debated fairly if we take the case of an actress whose lure is not beauty but some indecency of attitude, gesture or phrase, which is meant to awaken the debauchee keeping house in the breast of each of us with the ineffectual angel, and which either does this or bores us into the bar. (I do not, I may say, refer to Gaby Deslys, whom I, too, have not seen. I made more than one attempt, but the crush of beauty-lovers was too great.) It is quite easy to imagine an actress such as I have described: most of us have, in the course of many hours misspent in music-halls, seen her. To say that she may do good as well as harm is the same as saying that an indecent photograph may do good as well as harm. If this is to be the last word on the subject, then there is no logical reason why we should not decorate the walls of elementary schools with indecent photographs instead of maps, and teach the children limericks instead of *Lady Clara Vere de Vere* and *The Wreck of the Hesperus*. Mr Shaw may retort that he would allow any man who did not find indecent photographs and limericks "objectionable" to have his fill of them, but that he would not allow him to thrust them upon children. But this is to pass a moral judgment. If it is not certain whether the dangers of the sensual parodies of the arts are greater than the dangers of religion—or say, of geography—there is surely no more reason for preserving the children from one than from the other.

Even if we waive this point for the sake of argument, is Mr Shaw's other position tenable—that, if we consider any form of entertainment objectionable, we should show our disapproval, not by trying to have it stopped, but simply by staying away from it? Surely even in music-hall performances, there is a line to be drawn somewhere. We can no more be sure where good ends and evil begins than we can be sure where light ends and darkness begins. But we all have a good enough notion of when it is dark, and it is not so very difficult to tell when a music-hall turn is out of bounds. Some people, it may be granted, run to excess in their sense of propriety. They are as delicate as the lady who, when carving a chicken at table, used to inquire: "Will you have a wing or a limb?" On the other hand, there is an equally large number of people who have no delicacy at all but who are always ready to greet the obscene with a cheer. Their favourite meal of entertainment is brutality for an entrée and sensuality for a sweet. They can even mix their dishes at times, as, many years ago in Paris, when a woman stripped to the waist and with her hands tied behind her back used to get down on her knees and wait for rats to be loosed out of a cage and kill them one by one with her mouth. Is there no reason for suppressing a show of this kind except that it is rough on rats? I think there is. It deserves suppression because it is what we call, in a vague word, degrading. It is easy enough for a lively imagination to picture as beastly a scene in which there would be no rats present, and which, even if a thousand youths and maidens were willing to pay night after night to see it, would still be a case for the police.

One cannot help feeling that, in attacking the Bishop in regard to the liberty of music-halls, Mr Shaw has allowed himself to be made angry by the way in which the Church nearly always concentrates on sex when it wishes to make war on sin. Probably he does well to be angry. It is always worth while to denounce the Church for making morality so much an affair of abstinences. On the other hand, the Church and the prophets have realised by a wise instinct that this planet on which we live tends perpetually to become a huge disorderly house, and that the history of the world is largely the history of a struggle for decency. At times, no doubt, the world has also been in danger of being converted into a tyrannous Sabbath-school. But that was usually an aftermath of disorder. There is no denying that the average human being finds it far easier to learn to leer than to learn to sing psalms. The fight against the leer is one of the first necessities of civilisation. It may be argued that a policeman cannot be sent in pursuit of a leer as he can in search of a pickpocket, and that, if he were, he would more probably than not run it to earth in some masterpiece of art or literature. But what about the leer when it has been isolated—when it has no more connection with art or literature than with Esperanto?

Mr Shaw seems to think that even in that case the attempt to suppress it would be a form of persecution. But is it persecution to take action against pickpockets or against employers who dodge the Factory Acts or against the corrupters of children? Surely there are offences that are capable of being dealt with by magistrates. Only the most innocent optimist can believe that sweating, for instance, can be put an end to by public opinion in the abstract as effectively as it can be stopped by public opinion acting through the police. It is no argument to say that, if we suppress certain music-hall turns because we dislike them, those who object to the theory of the Atonement have an equal right to try to suppress the teaching and preaching of that doctrine. Might not the same argument be used against interference with thieves and forgers or still more extreme criminals in the pursuit of their livelihood? After all, supposing the Methodists added to the Calvinist and Wesleyan varieties already in existence a new sect of, say, Aphrodisiac Methodists, it is quite easy to conceive not only public opinion, but the police interfering with it with the approval of the mass of moral and immoral citizens. Similarly, if a sect of Particular Baptist Thugs made its appearance, its religious complexion would hardly save it from suppression. There might still be half-a-dozen apostles of religious freedom who would tell you that you could not logically take action against the Thugs and the Aphrodisiacs without preparing the way for the prohibition of Bible-reading and for burning psalm-singers at the stake. But common-sense knows better. It knows that there are certain things which must be put down, either by public opinion or by the police, if the world is to remain a place into which it is worth a child's while to be born. It knows, too, that the liberty to seek after truth and beauty in one's own way does not necessarily involve the liberty to say or to do whatever beastly thing one pleases, even if thousands of people enjoy it. If it did, then the Censor's interference with *Mrs Warren's Profession* would be an act of the same kind as Scotland Yard's interference with the worst kind of night clubs.

At the same time, one need not deny that the difficulty of deciding what should be suppressed and what should not is immense. I see that in some part of the world or other Isidora Duncan's dancing has been prohibited. I myself have met a lady, who, when she was taken to see Madame Duncan, was in an agony of blushes till she got out into the street. But she sat through *The Merry Widow* without turning a hair. What, then, is to be the test in these matters? On the whole I think it is a good rule to fight against the suppression of anything that can by any stretch of the imagination be considered honestly intended or beautiful. In the arts, one can believe without casuistry, beauty ultimately transforms the beast. But there are forms of art, literature and drama which are nothing else than a kind of indecent exposure. Let us give them the benefit of the doubt, so long as there is a doubt. But when there is no doubt, let them be given the benefit of the policeman.

I wonder whether Mr Shaw would have argued so fiercely on the other side if the Bishop had not dragged in the Censor. If the controversy had not got mixed up with the Censorship, indeed, it would have greatly simplified matters. Mr Shaw seems to have begun to belabour the Bishop from a feeling that a blow to the Bishop was a blow to the Censor, but having once begun, he seems to have gone on simply because he enjoyed beating a Bishop. And of the remains there were gathered up twelve basketsful. But, all the same, I cannot help feeling that the Bishop perished in a good cause.

IX
STUPIDITY

"Surely honest men may thank God they belong to 'the Stupid Party'!" — *The Spectator*, March 28, 1914.

It is a terrible thing to boast of stupidity, even in irony. It is a still more terrible thing to associate stupidity with honesty. There is a good deal to be said in favour of honesty, but stupidity in the garb of honesty is the merest masquerader. There was once a member of a local body whom I heard praised in the words: "He's the only honest man in the Corporation, and that is because he is too stupid to be anything else." I doubt if predestined honesty of this sort is entitled to a statue. It has its public uses, no doubt, as an occasional stumbling-block to those who traffic both in their own and other people's virtue. Here, at least, is virtue that cannot be bought at a crisis. On the other hand, it does not withstand the temptations of gold a bit more sturdily than it withstands the appeals of reason. It will not move either for a thousand pounds or for the Archangel Gabriel. It bars the way to Heaven and the road to Hell impartially. It has the unbudgeableness of the ass rather than the adaptability which enables human beings to survive on this wrinkled planet. Even so, one may admit a sneaking respect and affection for honest stupid people in private life. It is when they feel called upon to devote their combined honesty and stupidity to public affairs that one begins to tremble and to wonder whether, after all, an honest fool or a clever rogue is likely to do better service to the State. Oscar Wilde once said it was well that good people did not live to see the evil results of their goodness and that wicked people did not live to see the good results of their wickedness. This is true, perhaps, no matter how cunning one may be in one's virtue or how provident in one's vices. But it is especially true of that blind and bigoted honesty which cannot see farther than its nose. I know a town where the lamplighter twenty years ago was an honest old man of the blind and bigoted type. It was his duty to go out and light the lamps of the little town on every night when there was no moon. One month, however, it was noticed that all the lamps were alight while the moon was blazing, and that when the moon was dark the lamps were dark too. The old man was called before the town committee to account for his disobedience to orders. Instead of apologising, however, he firmly insisted that he had done his duty, and produced a calendar to prove that there was no moon on the nights on which everybody had seen it shining, and that it might have reasonably been expected to shine on the nights on which it was obscured. He was asked why he did not trust his eyes, but he said that he always went by the calendar, and he would not yield an inch of his position till someone took the calendar from him and noticed that it was not even a current one, but a calendar of the previous year. There, I think, is a dramatisation of a very common form of honesty. It is as common among Cabinet Ministers and Churchmen as among aged lamplighters. It expresses itself in adherence not only to antiquated Mother Seigel calendars but to constitutions and confessions of faith that have lost their meaning. Whether this can justly be called honesty at all is a question with something to be said on both sides. It is certainly stupidity of the very best quality.

One of the reasons why one rather disbelieves in reverencing stupidity is that it is not always as honest as it looks. It is often an armour instinctively, if not deliberately, put on by comfortable people. This kind of stupidity has sometimes been attributed to excessive eating and drinking, as when Holinshed wrote of the sixteenth-century Scots that "they far exceed us in overmuch and distemperate gormandise, and so engross their bodies that diverse of them do oft become unapt to any other purpose than to spend their times in large tabling and belly cheer." But I have known gluttons who have yet had all their wits about them and ladies who could hardly get through the wing of a chicken and were nevertheless as stupid as a prize cat blinking beside the fire. There is more in it than the stomach. Stupidity of the kind I mean is really an ingeniously built castle with moat and drawbridge to guard against the entrance of the facts of life—at least, of the disagreeable facts of life. It is by a perfect network of castles of this kind that so many feudal privileges have been kept alive generations after anyone defends the idea of feudalism. Against stupidity, it has been said, the gods themselves fight in vain, and it is hardly to be wondered at that democracy also falls back from the impassive walls of those old castles like a broken tide. It is only fair to say, however, that again and again different noble inmates—how suggestive a word—of the castles have refused to shelter themselves behind the drawbridge of stupidity and have even offered to lead the people in an assault on castles in general. It is then usually discovered that the people, too, have their dear retreat of stupidity to which they fly on the first hint of a raid upon Utopia. The stupidity of the underfed is an even more desperate thing than the stupidity of the overfed, and, when a castellan offers his sword to their cause, they merely look at each other and ask darkly: "What's he going to get out of it?" It is the popular stupidity which led Mr Shaw the other day to observe that he had more hope of converting a millionaire than a millionaire's chauffeur to Socialism. Certainly it is the stupid in the back streets who make the stupid in the castles secure. The latter see in the former, indeed, not only their first line of defence, but their justification. They see their justification, however, in everything and everybody. They wrap themselves up in little comforting thoughts that the poor do not feel things as the respectable do. I have heard a comfortable artist, for instance, in winter, arguing that there was no need to pity a blind beggar shivering at a street-corner. "Each of us is kept warm," he declared, "by a little stove in his stomach, and you would be surprised to know how little it takes to keep a man like that's stove alight. You see, he's been training himself all his life to do with very little food and very little clothing and to sit out in all kinds of weather. A fall in the temperature that would paralyse you or me would affect him hardly more than a fall in the price of champagne. You see, he's learned to do without things." There was almost a note of envy in his voice for the man who had learned to do without things—without soap, and meat, and blankets, and clothes-brushes, and servants, and fires, and sunshine. That seems to be one of the favourite hypocrisies of the stupid, the pretence of envying the poor. I have seen a merchant grow suddenly eloquent as he described the happy lot of the working-man, who had nothing to do but draw his wages, and compared it with the anxious life of the employer, who had all the cares and responsibilities of the business on his shoulders. The rich never feel so good as when they are speaking of their possessions as responsibilities. Hear a mistress set forth the advantages of the life of a servant-girl—how she not only gets higher wages than servants ever got before, but think of the food, and no rent to pay! She even becomes mawkish over the fortune of a girl who is too poor to be called upon to pay rates and taxes. Alas, these idylls of the kitchen are all written in the drawing-room. If a servant's life were all a matter of freedom from rent and rates and taxes and the worries of making both ends meet on a thousand a year, the idylls would be apt enough; but it is just possible that even to make both ends meet on twenty-five pounds a year may have its own difficulties. Certainly one has a right to suspect these ladies who glorify the life of the cook and the parlour-maid. I will refuse to believe in them till I hear that one of them has run away from her husband to take one of those sinecures advertised in the domestic service columns of the *Morning Post*. But, perhaps, their sense of duty is too strong to allow them to fly from their responsibilities in that way.

Stupidity might be defined as resignation to other people's misfortunes. Alternatively, it is a way of regarding comforts as responsibilities and of getting out of one's uncomfortable responsibilities altogether. There is no greater enemy of change. For, granted enough stupidity, it is easy to believe that Hell itself is Heaven. It is the stupidity of the rich, rather than deliberate heartlessness, that permits so many of them to live cheerfully on ill-paid labour and slum rents. Fortunately the cheerful dullness of rich people is rarer than it was a century ago. Then it was reinforced by political economy which regarded transactions in human beings in much the same light as transactions in pounds of tea. Our first awakening to the right of other people to live happened just before we gave up cannibalism. The second happened just before we gave up slavery. The third will happen just before we give up capitalism. Obviously, it is only our stupidity which enables us to go on putting the rights of Tom, Dick, and Harry before the rights of the race. It is only our stupidity which makes us believe that, while it is right that superfluous wealth should be taxed a shilling in the pound for the good of all, it would be robbery to tax it ten shillings in the pound for the good of all. The first statesman who levied the first tax thereby announced the dual ownership of property between the citizen and the State. He vindicated the right of the State, representing the common good, as against the individual, representing only his private good, to a first share in property. The income-tax stands for exactly the same principle in regard to State rights as would the nationalisation of the land or the railways. As we grow less stupid, we shall gradually awake to the fact that there is no right to food and shelter and State benevolence that we possess which our neighbours ought not also in justice to possess. We shall gradually understand, for instance, that it is not worth while that a thousand children should be brought up in the gutters of misery in order that a few dozen young gentlemen may sup on plovers' eggs. It has already dawned upon us that, if pensions are good for field-marshals, they cannot be so very bad for linen-lappers. Perhaps we shall yet come to see that a pension is a very good thing to begin life with as well as to end life with. In the meantime, most of us are either too comfortable or too miserable to think about such things. Our stupidity, at least, keeps conscience or revolution from destroying the peace of our meals.

X
WASTE

When Mr Churchill referred in Manchester to the piling up of armaments as so much misdirected human energy, he said something with which men of all parties will agree, except those few romantic souls who believe that it is a bracing thing to shed the blood of a foreigner every now and then. Obviously, if two men live beside one another, and if each of them is so afraid of the other's climbing secretly into his back garden that he hires a watchman to walk up and down the garden path all day and night with a six-shooter in his hand, he is wasting on his fears a great deal of energy that might be expended on cabbages. Again, if there is a stream running between the gardens, and if each of the householders is always preparing for the day when the other may question his right to use the water, he will have to hire other strong men, and many a man who might have made a good blacksmith or barman may be turned into a sailor. The situation is so absurd that it does not bear thinking about except as a game: the military aristocracies who treat preparation for war as a form of sport are in this entirely logical. On the other hand, when the burgess fulminates against war as though it were the only example of wasted human energy that does not bear thinking of, he is shutting his eyes to the fact that the whole of modern civilisation is built upon a foundation of waste where it is not built upon a foundation of want.

Our estimates of men and nations rise and fall with their capacity for waste. The great nation, in the eyes of the Imperialist, is the nation that can waste the world. It is the nation that can mow down harvests of savages without even the comparatively decent excuse that it wants to eat them. It is the nation that can make the genius of other nations as though it were not—that can ruin harbours and send ships worth a million pounds to the bottom of the sea. I do not say that there are not other elements that have a part in the greatness of nations. But the power of destruction alone is enough to make any nation supreme for a day—and the supremacy of no nation lasts much longer—and remembered in history. Similarly, with individual men and women. "Everybody," said Emerson, "loves a lover." It would be almost truer to say that everybody loves a wastrel. In our boyhood we love those who waste themselves. In our discreeter years we envy those who can waste the lives of others. It has often been noticed that youths and maidens have a tenderness for drunkards and rakes. They reverence the genius of life wasted almost more than the genius of life fulfilled. Byron, whose vices killed him in his thirties; Sydney Carton, who was seldom sober; Mr Kipling's gentleman-rankers, "damned from here to eternity" — these awake a passionate devotion in the breasts of the young such as is never lavished on successful grocers. It is the prodigal son, and not his respectable brother, at whom affectionate eyes look round as he passes along the street. Perhaps it is because he is so much more obviously trying a fall with destiny than the grocer. The mark of doom makes a more picturesque effect on the brow than a silk-lined bowler hat. According to this view, the wastrel owes his appeal largely to the fact that he is a fighter in a lost cause — the cause of those who have lifted hands against the universe.

The reverence of middle age for the wealthier geniuses of waste, however, cannot be explained on grounds like these. One does not think of Lord Tomnoddy or Sir Alexander Soapsuds as a warrior against destiny. The prodigality of the rich appeals to us for quite other reasons than does the prodigality of the prodigal. We endure it chiefly because we envy it. The dream of being a rich man who can thrust out men and women from their homes to make room for pheasants, who by sheer economic pressure can force us to make bonbons for his guests when we ought to be making boots for ourselves, who can take a man who might be a duke and turn him into a flunkey, lulls us into a kind of satisfaction with the world. The man who has the power to waste fields and men and women and money and labour is the king who rules in every vulgar heart among us. His royal wastefulness in food and servants and ornaments brings him, it may be granted, not a teaspoonful of added health or an eggcupful more of happiness. Even the poets, who have so often sung for rich masters, have always had the grace to warn them that over-eating and over-drinking and over-confidence in this world's goods were merely three death's-heads dressed up in seductive bonnets. But the truth is we never believe the poets when once we have laid down the book. Our ideal of wastefulness is firmly rooted in us beyond the attacks of any æsthete with his harmless little quiver of phrases.

Even when we are not rich ourselves we can imitate the rich in their wastefulness. There is nothing the average servant scorns more than the house in which she is expected to make use of the torsos of loaves, and in which she is forbidden to sacrifice odds and ends of meat to the little gods of the dust-bin. She loves the house where there is milk for the sink as well as for the children and the cat. Years ago, when some people were advocating a tax on salt, they did so on the ground that no one need suffer since at present everybody puts on his plate several times as much salt as he ever uses. Hence, if we were more careful with the salt, such a tax would be a tax not on salt but on wastefulness. It is the same with mustard. I remember a Scotsman once asking me in a hushed voice if I knew how Colman had made his fortune. I thought from my friend's solemn air that it must have been in some sensational way—by buying a deserted gold-mine or running a South American revolution. But my friend merely pointed to the plate from which I was eating. "He made it," he declared solemnly, "out of mustard you leave on the edge of your plate."

Perhaps the Scotsman was right in shaking his head so gravely over our extravagance in mustard. But somehow I, too, have the kitchen's taste for superfluities, and enough never seems half so good as a little more. Horace described the happy man as the man who had enough and something over for servants and thieves. "Oh, the little more, and how much it is!" Even if we grudge it to the thieves, we love it because of the sense it gives us that we are no longer struggling in the water but sitting in triumph on the dry land. The average Englishman dislikes Tariff Reform, not entirely because he has grasped the economics of the subject, but because it would bring in a system which would compel him to be as thrifty as a Frenchman and as careful as a German. One must admit to a certain degree of sympathy with him. When one hears of French peasants (as I once did) calling round after the meals of the rich to carry off the scrapings of the plates to make soup for their families, and of their doing this not because they were very poor, but because they were very thrifty, one's heart suddenly rejoices at the sight of the tattered old flag of prodigality again. One does not want to see thrift given the extreme character of an orgy.

On the other hand, a good many of us get an easy sense of the heroic by living in lordly wastefulness. It appeals to us as a kind of enlargement of our personality. That is why so many of us shrink with horror from such social economies as a kitchen or a heating apparatus that would serve a street. We like our own fires and our own bad cookery. It is as childish as if we wanted our own footpath and our own moon, and no doubt we would insist on these if we could. We pretend that romance would leave the world if the sausages were turned by a citizen in a municipal cap of liberty instead of by a wage-slave, and that freedom would be dead if we warmed our toes at a civic fire. I wonder that no one takes exception to the communal warmth of the sun.

The present wastefulness would be little worse than an insane joke if all this multiplying of cooks and parlourmaids did not absorb such an amount of reluctant youth and deftness and energy. But, alas! our ideals of private citizenship seldom mean that we do our work privately ourselves. They only mean that we privately hire somebody else to do it. In other words, they are usually a violation of the private citizenship of somebody else. Consequently, though we enjoy helping in the wastefulness of it all as a puppy enjoys tearing a book, we do not feel justified in elevating our tastes into an ethical system. We are simply grabbers of the corn supply. Probably, even in a hundred years, people will look back on our present west-European society and marvel at the common habit of prosperous men in sitting down to a table where there are far more dishes and elegancies than they can ever absorb, while men, women and children walk the streets empty. I seldom sit down to dinner in a hotel without a sense that I am being offered three people's food. No, a society that gives three people's food to one man and one man's portion of food—or less—to three people must be the laughing-stock of angels. The social waste that results from railway monopolies and battleship programmes and the warren of small shops in every city is as nothing to this. Except, perhaps, in so far as it is the cause of this. On the whole, however, the problem of waste goes deeper than battleships, which are but toys and which will disappear as soon as the nations grow up and cease making faces at each other. It is a problem on the same level with lust, which, indeed, is a form of waste. It is one of the great problems of egoism, which is more concerned with mastery than with truth or common-sense or gentleness. Not mastery of oneself—just gimcrack, made-in-Birmingham mastery. This is the Mammon of our conceit upon whose altars we are willing to offer up the sacrifice of the wasted earth.

XI
ON CHRISTMAS

There is a cant of Christmas, and there is a cant of anti-Christmas. There are some people who want to throw their arms round you simply because it is Christmas; there are other people who want to strangle you simply because it is Christmas. Thus, between those who appreciate and those who depreciate Christmas, it is difficult for an ordinary man to escape bruises. As I grow older, I confess, I accept Christmas more philosophically than I used to do. There was a time when it seemed a dangerous institution, like home life or going to church. One felt that in undermining its joys one was making a breach in the defences of an ancient hypocrisy. Still more, one resented the steady boredom of the day—the boredom of a day from which one had been led to expect larger ecstasies than a surfeit of dishes and the explosion of crackers can give. One might have enjoyed it well enough, perhaps, if one had not had the feeling that it was one's duty to be happy. But to be deliberately happy for a whole day was a task as exhausting as deliberately hopping with one's feet tied. It was not that one wanted to be unhappy. It was merely that one desired one's liberty to be either as happy or as miserable as one pleased.

Remembering these early hostilities, I will not bid anyone be happy or merry or jolly on Christmas Day, except as the turkey and plum-pudding move them. At the same time, I cannot let the festival pass without recanting my childish insolence towards the holly and the mistletoe. I have been converted to Christmas as thoroughly almost as that prince of individualists, Scrooge. I can now pull a cracker with any man; I can accept gifts without actual discourtesy; and if the flame goes out before the plum-pudding reaches me, I am as mortified as can be. The Christmas tree shines with the host of the stars, and I can even forgive my neighbour who plays "While shepherds watched" all day long on the gramophone. The Salvation Army, which plays the same tune and one or two others all through the small hours on the trombone and the cornet-à-piston, is a severer test of endurance. But even that one can grin and bear when one remembers that the Salvationist bandsmen are but a sort of melancholy herald angels. The solitary figure in the Christmas procession, indeed, whom one hates with a boiling and bubbling hatred, is the postman who does not call. In Utopia the postman does not miss a letter-box on Christmas Day. Or on any other day.

It would be affectation to pretend, however, that one has suddenly developed a craving for plum-pudding and cracker-mottoes in one's middle age. One's reconcilement with Christmas is due neither to one's stomach nor to a taste for the wit and wisdom of cracker manufacturers. It is simply that one has come to enjoy a season of lordly inutility, when for the space of a day or two the cash-nexus hangs upon the world as light as air. It is no small thing to have this upsetting of the tyrannies, if it is only for a few hours. The heathen, as we call them, realised this even before the birth of Christ, and had the Saturnalia and other festivals of the kind in which a communism of licence ruled, if not a communism of gentleness. It is still an instinct in many Christian places to turn Christmas into a general orgy—to make it a day on which one bows down and worships the human maw. (And there are worse things in the world than brandy-sauce.) On the other hand, there is also the instinct to make of the day a door into a new world of neighbourliness. It is the only day in the year on which many men speak humanly to their servants and open their eyes to the cheerful lives of children and simple people. Hypercritical youth will deny that man has a right to confine his neighbourliness to a single day in the year any more than he has a right to confine his sanctity to the Sabbath. But we who have ceased to exact miracles from human nature are glad to have even a single day as a beginning. Socialism, we may admit, depends upon the extension of the Christmas festival into the rest of the year. It demands that the relations between man and man shall be, as far as possible, not shopkeeping relations, but Christmas relations. In other words, it aims at a society in which the little conquests of gain will cease to be the chief end of time, and men will no more think of cheating each other than Romeo would think of cheating Juliet. Nor is there any other side of the new civilisation which will be more difficult to build than this. This is the very spirit of the new city. Without it the rest would be but a chaos of stones and mortar—a Gehenna of purposeless machinery.

It is an extraordinary fact that the rediscovery of Christmas in the nineteenth century was not followed sooner by the rediscovery of the limitations of individualism. Dickens himself, the incarnation of Christmas, did not realise till quite late in life what a denial modern civilisation is of the Christmas spirit. Even in *Hard Times*, where, as Mr Shaw pointed out, he expresses the insurrection of the human conscience against a Manchesterised society, he offers us no hope except from the spread of a sort of Tory benevolence. Perhaps, however, it does not matter how you label benevolence so long as it is the real thing and is not merely another name for that most insidious form of egotism—patronage. That Dickens was pugnaciously benevolent in all his work—except when he was writing about Dissenters and Americans—was one of the most fortunate accidents in the popular literature of the nineteenth century. He did not, perhaps, dramatise the secret mystery of human brotherhood—the brotherhood of saint and fool and criminal and ordinary man—as Tolstoi and Dostoevsky have done in some of their work. But he dramatised goodwill with a thoroughness never attempted before in England.

On the whole, it may be doubted whether the Christmas spirit has not grown stronger and deeper since the time of Dickens. Only a few years ago it seemed as though it were dying. People began to detest even Christmas cards as something more Victorian than *The Idylls of the King*. But here the old enthusiasm is back again, and we can no more kill Christmas than the lion could kill Androcles. Perhaps the popularisation of Italian art, as well as Dickens, has something to do with it. Our imaginations cannot escape from the Virgin and the Child, and we are like children ourselves in the inquisitiveness with which we peer into that magic stable where the ass and the cow worship and the shepherds and the kings and the little angels in their nightgowns are on their knees. There has come back a gaiety, a playfulness, into the picture, such as our grandfathers might have thought irreverent, but their grandfathers' grandfathers, on the other hand, would have seen to be perfectly natural. The cult of the child has, perhaps, been overdone in recent years, and we have brought our mawkishness and our morbid analysis even to the side of the cradle. At the same time, no one has yet been able to point out a way by which we can escape from the obsession of rates and taxes, of profit and loss, except by the recovery of the child's vision. Without that vision religion itself becomes a matter of profit and loss. With that vision the dullest world blossoms with flowers; even truisms cease to be meaningless; and Christmas is itself again. Out of the drowning of the world we have made a toy for the nursery, and the birth of the King of Glory has become the theme of a song for infants.

One of the most exquisite pictures in literature is that of the three ships that come sailing into Bethlehem "on Christmas Day, in the morning"; and not less childishly beautiful is that other short carol:

> There comes a ship far sailing then,
> Saint Michael was the steersman,
> Saint John sat in the horn;
> Our Lord harped, our Lady sang,
> And all the bells of Heaven they rang,
> On Christ's Sunday at morn.

One sees the same childish imagination at work in the old English carol, "Hail, comely and clean," in which the three shepherds come to the inn stable with their gifts, the first with "a bob of cherries" for the new-born baby, the second with a bird, and the third with a tennis-ball. "Hail," cries the third shepherd—

> Hail, darling dear, full of godheed!
> I pray Thee be near, when that I have need.
> Hail! sweet Thy cheer! My heart would bleed
> To see Thee sit here in so poor weed,
> With no pennies.
> Hail! put forth Thy dall!
> I bring Thee but a ball,
> Have and play Thee withal.
> And go to the tennis.

These songs, it may be, are more popular to-day than they were fifty years ago—partly owing to the decline of the old-fashioned suspicious sort of Protestantism, which saw the Pope behind every bush—including the holly-bush. One remembers how Protestants of the old school used to denounce even Raphael's grave Madonnas as trash of Popery. "I'll have no Popish pictures in my house," declared a man I know to his son, who had brought home the Sistine Madonna to hang on his walls; and the picture had to be given away to a friend. Similarly, the observance of Christmas Day was regarded in some places as a Popish superstition. One old Protestant clergyman many years ago used to make the rounds of his friends and parishioners on Christmas morning to wish them the compliments of the day. It was his custom, however, to pray with each of them, and in the course of his prayers to explain that he must not be regarded as taking Christmas Day seriously. "Lord," he would pray, "we are not gathered here in any superstitious spirit, as the Roman Catholics are, under the delusion that Thy Son was born in Bethlehem on the twenty-fifth of December. Hast not Thou told us in Thy Holy Book that on the night on which Thy Son was born the shepherds watched their flocks by night in the open air? And Thou knowest, O Lord, that in the fierce and inclement weather of December, with its biting frosts and its whirling snows, this would not have been possible, and can be but a Popish invention." But, having set himself right with God, he was human enough to proceed on his journey of good wishes. Noble intolerance like his is now, I believe, dead. To-day even a Plymouth Brother may wreathe his brow with mistletoe, and a Presbyterian may wish you a merry Christmas without the sky or the Shorter Catechism falling.

XII
ON DEMAGOGUES

It is still the custom in civilised countries for the politicians to call each other names. The word "serpent" has, one regrets to say, fallen out of use. But we are compensated for this in some measure by the invention of new terms of insult almost every day. It is not very long since Mr Lloyd George called Mr Steel Maitland "the cat's-meat-man of the Tory party," and Mr Steel Maitland retorted by calling Mr Lloyd George "Gehazi, the leper." And, side by side with original fancies of this kind, the old-fashioned dictionary of abuse still stands as open as the English Bible, where statesmen may arm themselves with nouns and adjectives that everybody can understand, such as "duke," "turncoat," "Jack Cade," "paid agitator," "Irish," "attorney," "despot," "nefarious" (which was almost as dead as "serpent" till Sir Edward Carson revived it), and, last but not least, "demagogue." It is only a day or two since Mr Bonar Law called Mr Lloyd George a demagogue, and one was disappointed to find that Mr Lloyd George, instead of calling Mr Bonar Law Nebuchadnezzar or Judas Iscariot in return, merely insisted that he could not be a demagogue, because a demagogue was a man who kicked away the ladder by which he had risen. This is very much as if you were to call a man "Bill Sikes," and he retorted that he could not be Bill Sikes because Bill Sikes had a wooden leg. Of course, Bill Sikes had not a wooden leg, and a demagogue is not necessarily a man who kicks away the ladder by which he has risen. A demagogue is simply a mob-leader—a man who appeals to popular passions rather than principles. He is what half the statesmen of all parties aspire to be in every democratic community. Despots obtain their mastery over the crowd by the sword: demagogues by the catchword. That is the difference between a tyranny and a democracy. It may not seem to be a change for the better to those who have a taste for the costumes and lights of the theatre. But the demagogue at least consults the mob as though it had a mind and will of its own. The very way in which he flatters it and instigates it to passion is an assertion of its freedom of choice, and, therefore, a concession to the dignity of human nature. It is like wooing as compared with marriage by capture.

Even when we have put the demagogue securely above the despot, however, we are left in considerable doubt about him. Somehow or other we do not like him. We do not trust him further than we can see him. We distrust him as Aristophanes, Shakespeare, and Dickens did. We feel that the difference between a demagogue and a statesman is that the former converts human beings into a mob, while the latter exalts a mob into a company of human beings. It is the difference between a pander and a prophet. It is true that men of a conservative temper hate the pander and the prophet almost equally. Shakespeare, for instance, who was a bad politician as well as a good poet, mocks at Utopias no less than at bombast in that unhistorical picture he suggests of Jack Cade:—

> Cade: There shall be in England seven halfpenny loaves sold for a penny: the three-hooped pot shall have ten hoops, and I will make it felony to drink small beer: all the realm shall be in common; and in Cheapside shall my palfrey go to grass; and when I am king, as king I will be,——
>
> All: God save your majesty!
>
> Cade: I thank you, good people: there shall be no money; all shall eat and drink on my score; and I will apparel them all in one livery, that they may agree like brothers, and worship me, their lord.
>
> Dick: The first thing we do, let's kill all the lawyers.
>
> Cade: Nay, that I mean to do.

To many of us, if you omit Cade's occasional lapses into individualism—as in his desire to be worshipped as a king—this will seem an admirable programme. It will more than hold its own in comparison with any programme that ever originated in Newcastle or Birmingham. William Morris himself might have had that vision of restoring Cheapside to green fields, and even the extremest Marconoclast could hardly go further than Cade in suggestions for a summary way with lawyers. Who is there who is not whole-heartedly with Cade for the abolition of poverty? In fact, there seems little to criticise in the man as Shakespeare drew him, except that he made his proposals for personal, not for social ends. That, I believe, is the real essence of demagogy.

To be a demagogue is not to advocate one thing rather than another. It depends on the manner, not on the matter, of one's proposals. One may reap one's own glory out of praise of the New Jerusalem no less than out of the most vulgar incitements to war and hatred. It is a temptation to which every man is subject who has ever stood on a cart above a crowd of his fellows. One feels tempted to play on them, like a child who finds itself left alone with a piano. It is worse than that. A crowd is like a sea of liquor, the fumes of which go to an orator's head and make him boast and lie and leer as he would be ashamed to see himself doing in his sober senses. He becomes, to parody Novalis on Spinoza, a mob-intoxicated man. But there is one notable difference between a decent drunkard and a demagogue. The drunkard is satisfied with getting drunk himself. The demagogue is not content till he has made the crowd drunk too. He and the mob are, as it were, mutual intoxicants, and in the result many a public meeting turns into so disgraceful an orgy that, if anything comparable to it occurred in a music-hall, the licence would be withdrawn. This is a kind of vice of which the moralists have not yet taken sufficient note. And yet there is no more execrable passion on earth than demagogue-passion on the one hand, and mob-passion on the other. Cleon will always be remembered as one of the basest Athenians who ever lived, and this is because he was the first demagogue of Imperialism—a violent animal on his hind-legs who bellowed till he woke up the blood-lust of his fellow-citizens. He was powerful only so long as he could keep that and other popular lusts active. Men, it has been said by a notable philosopher, seek after power rather than beauty; but this, I believe, is only true of demagogues and egoists of kindred sorts. The demagogue is the man who, instead of aiming at bringing the mob to his mood, feels after the mood of the mob, and, having discovered it, whips it into froth and fury. If you keep your eyes open at a public meeting—not always an easy thing to do in days when men discuss Welsh Disestablishment—you will see how the demagogue often becomes the master of a meeting that has listened coldly to intelligent and honest speeches. Like pot-boiling in art, it is perfectly easy if you know the way. The Sausage Seller who aspired to be Cleon's rival, in *The Knights* of Aristophanes, expounds the whole art of demagogy in his prayer:

> Ye influential impudential powers
> Of sauciness and jabber, slang and jaw!|
> Ye spirits of the market-place and street,
> Where I was reared and bred—befriend me now!
> Grant me a voluble utterance, and a vast
> Unbounded voice, and steadfast impudence!

And, in another passage, Demosthenes initiates him into the means of obtaining power over the people:

> Interlard your rhetoric with lumps
> Of mawkish sweet, and greasy flattery.
> Be fulsome, coarse, and bloody!

This, indeed, is what oratory is bound to degenerate into in a democracy unless it is the weapon of a conviction. It is like any other form of art which is practised, not from any burning and generous motive, but for mere love of that sense of power which gain and popularity give. Dickens, owing to a curious gap in his knowledge, made his typical Trade-Union leader, Slackbridge, in *Hard Times*, a demagogue of the ranting type, who began a speech:

> Oh, my friends, the down-trodden operatives of Coketown! Oh, my friends and fellow-countrymen, the slaves of an iron-handed and a grinding despotism! Oh, my friends and fellow-sufferers, and fellow-workmen and fellow-men!

Slackbridge, we are also told, was "an ill-made, high-shouldered man with lowering brows, and his features crushed into an habitually sour expression." That represents the attitude of many people to popular leaders. They believe that no one can advocate a reasonable future for the poor without being venomous and of an ugly appearance. They do not realise that the demagogues and agitators of to-day are chiefly men of the propertied classes and their allies, like Sir Edward Carson and Mr F.E. Smith. Sir Edward Carson's speeches in Ulster, indeed, are the most extreme instances of demagogy we have had in recent years. They are all noise and passion, roaring echoes of the mob-soul, rhetoric and not reason, thunderstorms instead of light. They are appeals to the war-spirit—the same spirit that Cleon and all the demagogues have sought to awaken. Incidentally I admit that a class-war or a sex-war may as readily produce its Carsons as a war of sectarianism. Sir Edward Carson is the awful example to all creeds and classes of how not to do it.

XIII
ON COINCIDENCES

An amazing story of coincidences appears in the *Westminster Gazette*. During the Boer War four men met by chance for the first time on the eve of some big action, and the meeting was so agreeable that one of the men who had a bad two-shilling piece in his pocket divided it, and gave each of the others a quarter as a memento of the evening. Immediately afterwards they separated, and never saw or heard of each other again till a few evenings ago, when a dinner was given in honour of somebody or other in Birmingham. The four men were friends of the guest of the evening, and all of them turned up at the dinner, where they recognised each other easily, we are told, because each of them was wearing his quarter-florin on his watch-chain.

Life is, of course, a series of coincidences, but we never cease to be surprised as each new one happens, and nothing can destroy their recurring freshness. We may make mathematical calculations showing that there is a chance in a million that such and such a thing will happen, but, when it happens once in a million times, it seems to us as marvellous as a comet. We cannot get accustomed to the pattern of Nature, which repeats itself as daringly as the pattern in a wall-paper. Our fathers recognised this pattern, and saw in it the weird craftsmanship of destiny. We who believe in iron law, which surely implies a rigid pattern, are by a curious want of logic sceptics, and we treat each new emergence of the pattern as a strange exception to scientific rule. We cannot believe that Nature arranged howlings of dogs and disasters in the stars to accompany the death of a Cæsar or a Napoleon. Everything that we can call dramatic in Nature we put down to chance and coincidence. Superstitious people confront us with instance upon instance of the succession of omen and event, but we label these exception No. 1, exception No. 2, and so forth, and go cheerfully on our way.

Believers in omens tell us that, some time before Laud's trial and execution, he found his portrait fallen on to the floor, and predicted disaster; and they ask us to admit that this was more than a coincidence, especially as there are a hundred similar stories. They relate how the stumble of a horse proved as fatal an omen for Mungo Park as did the fall of a picture for Laud. One day before he departed on his last expedition to Africa his horse stumbled, and Sir Walter Scott, who was with him, said: "I am afraid this is a bad omen." "Omens follow those who look to them," replied the explorer, and set forth on the expedition from which he never returned. Luckily we have examples which suggest that Park and not Scott was right. Everyone knows the story of William the Conqueror's fall as he landed on the shores of England, and how, in order to calm the superstitious alarm of his followers, he called on them to observe how he had taken possession of the country with both hands. In the very fact of doing so, of course, he merely substituted one interpretation of an omen for another. But if omens are capable in this way of opposite interpretations, we are on the direct road to scepticism about their significance, and so to a view that most events that appear to have been heralded by omens are simple coincidences.

One remarkable coincidence of this kind came to my ears the other day. A man I know was suddenly dismissed from his post with three months' salary in his pocket. I happened to be talking about superstitions with him the same afternoon, when he said: "It's all very well, but only last week, when I was in the country, some one was telling fortunes by tea-leaves in the house where I was stopping; and he turned to me and said: 'Old man, there's a big surprise in store for you, and I see some money in the bottom of the cup.' I shan't let them know this has happened," he added, "as it might encourage them to be superstitious." Certainly, when such a coincidence happens in our own lives, it is difficult to believe that it is not a deliberate act on the part of Nature. Nature, we can see, does concern herself with the minutest cell or atom of our being; why not with these premonitory shadows of our deeds and sufferings? Many coincidences, on the other hand, admit of a less fatalistic explanation. Everybody has noticed how one no sooner meets a new name in a book that one comes on the same name in real life also for the first time. I had not read Mr Forrest Reid's novel, *The Bracknels*, a week, when, on walking down a London avenue, the same name—"The Bracknels"—stared at me from a gate. It is not easy, however, to conceive that destiny deliberately leads one into a suburban avenue to enjoy the humour of one's surprise at so trivial a coincidence. It is a more natural conclusion that these names one begins to notice so livelily would still have remained unobserved, were it not that they had acquired a new significance for one's eyes owing to something one had read or heard. After all, one can ride down the Strand on the top of a 'bus for a month without consciously seeing a single name over a shop-window. But let any of these names become real to us as the result of some accident, and it leaps to one's eyes like a scene in a play. It is merely that one now selects this particular name for observation, and ignores the others. It is all due to the artistic craving for patterns. I am inclined at times to explain the evidence in favour of the Baconian theory of Shakespeare as pattern-mongering. Those cyphers, those coincidences of phrase and suggestion at such-and-such a line from the beginning or end of so many of the plays, those recurrences of hoggish pictures, are enough to shake the balance of anyone who cannot himself go forward with a study of the whole evidence. But, as we proceed with an examination of the coincidences, we find that many of them are coincidences only for the credulous. It seems a strange coincidence that Shakespeare and Bacon should so often make use of the same metaphors and words. But it seems strange only till we discover that plenty of other pre-Shakespearean and Elizabethan writers made use of them as well. Much of the Baconian theory, indeed, is built, not upon coincidence, but upon pseudo-coincidence. The fact that Shakespeare died on the same day of the month—or almost on the same day—as that on which he was born is really a more interesting coincidence than any that occurs within the field of Baconianism.

Much the same may be said of the coincidences discovered by those who have, at one time or another, counted up the numerical values of the letters in the names of Napoleon and Gladstone and other leaders of men, and found that they were equal to 666, the fatal number of the Antichrist. In nearly every case the name has been distorted in its transliteration into Greek in such a way as to make the coincidence no coincidence at all. On the other hand, there are some genuinely interesting coincidences in figures, which have been recorded by various writers on credulity and superstition. French history since the middle of the eighteenth century can almost be written as a series of figure-mongers' coincidences. It began with Louis XVI, who came to the throne in 1774. By adding the sum of the ciphers in this figure to the figure itself—1774+1+7+7+4—the arithmetical diviners point out that you get 1793, the year of the King's death. Similarly, the beginning of the French Revolution foretold the end of the Revolutionary period with Napoleon's fall, for if you add up 1789+1+7+8+9 you get 1814, the year of Elba. Louis Philippe's accession-date, 1830, gives scarcely less remarkable results. If you add to it the figures in 1773, the date of his birth—1830+1+7+7+3—you get 1848, the date of his fall and flight. It is the same if you add to his accession-date the figures in 1809, the date of his marriage. Here again 1830+1+8+0+9 results in 1848. And, if you turn to his Queen, you find that the figures in her birth-date, 1782, lead up to the same fatal message: 1830+1+7+8+2 once more mount to the ominous figure. The arithmeticians, whose ingenuities are recorded in Mr Sharper Knowlson's *Origins of Popular Superstitions*, have unearthed similar significances in the dates of Napoleon III. They add the figure 1852—the date of his inauguration as Emperor—to the ciphers of 1808, his birth-date—1852+1+8+0+8—and arrive at the fatal date, 1869, when the Empire came to an end. The Empress Eugénie was born in 1826 and married in 1853. Add the ciphers in these dates to 1852—1852+1+8+5+3 or+1+8+2+6—and 1869 appears once more. But there is no need to go on with these quaint sums. I have quoted enough to suggest the intricate and subtle patterns which the ingenious can discover everywhere in Nature.

Nature, assuredly, has provided us with coincidences so lavishly that we may well go about in amazement. Even the fiction of Mr William Le Queux is not quite so abundant in strange coincidences as the life of the most ordinary man you could see reading a halfpenny newspaper. It is only in literature, indeed, that coincidences seem unnatural. Sophocles has been blamed for making a tragedy out of a man who unwittingly slew his father and afterwards unwittingly married his mother. It is incredible as fiction; but I imagine real life could give us as startling a coincidence even as that. Each of us is, to use Sir Thomas Browne's phrase, Africa and its prodigies. We tread a miraculous earth which is all mirrors and echoes, hints and symbols and correspondences. Each deed we do may, for all we know, be echoed and mirrored in Nature in a thousand places, even before we do it, and I can imagine it possible that the shape of a man's fate may be scattered over the palm of his hand. I am a sceptic on the subject, and I see what a door is opened to charlatanry if we admit the presence of too many meanings in the world about us. But I am not ready to deride the notion that there may be some undiscovered law underlying many of the coincidences which puzzle us. True, if someone contended that a mysterious sort of gravitation was working steadily through the years to bring those four soldiers together again at the Birmingham dinner, I should be anxious to hear his proofs. But I am willing to listen patiently to almost any theory on the subject. No theory could be more sensational than the facts.

XIV
ON INDIGNATION

There is nothing in which the newspapers deal more generously than indignation. There is enough indignation going to waste in the columns of the London Press to overturn the Pyramids in ruins and to alter the course of the Danube. We have had a characteristic flow of popular indignation over the execution of Mr Benton, a British citizen, in Mexico. Probably not one Englishman in a million had ever heard of Mr Benton before, but no sooner was he executed and in his grave than he rose, as it were, the very impersonation of British citizenship outraged by foreigners. On the whole, there is nothing healthier than group-indignation of the kind that sees in an injury to one an injury to all—that demands just dealing for even the poorest and least distinguished member of the group. It is the sort of passion it would be pleasant to see trained and developed. My only complaint against it is that in the present state of the world it is too often reserved for foreigners and for those semi-foreigners, the people who belong to a different political party or social class from your own. One would have thought, for instance, that the group-indignation which denounced the execution of Mr Benton without a fair trial might also have denounced the expulsion of the labour leaders from South Africa with no trial at all. The fact that it did not and that several of the London capitalist papers treated the whole South African episode as a good joke at the expense of Labour is evidence that to a good many Englishmen the maltreatment of British citizens is not in itself an objectionable thing, provided it happens within the British Empire. It seems to me that this is an entirely topsy-turvy kind of patriotism. For every British citizen who is likely to be badly treated abroad, there must be thousands who are in danger of being badly treated in the British Empire itself. Is not the killing of an Englishman by an English railway company, for instance, as outrageous a crime as the killing of an Englishman by a foreign general? There is also this to be remembered: your indignation against the criminal in your own country is more likely to bear fruit than your indignation against the criminal in a foreign country. You can catch your English railway-director with a single policeman; you may not be able to catch your foreigner without an international war. Thus, though I do not question the occasional value of indignation against wicked foreigners, I contend that a true economy of indignation would lead to most of its being directed against wicked fellow-countrymen.

It may be retorted that Englishmen certainly do not limit their indignation to foreigners, and that the Marconi campaign is a proof that a good Englishman can always become righteously indignant against a bad Englishman—at least when the latter happens to be a Welshman or a Jew. But the Marconi campaign was only another example of group-indignation against persons who were outside the group. It was not, in this instance, a national or Imperial group: it was a party group. What I am arguing for is the direction of group-indignation, not against outsiders, but when necessary against the members of the group. I should like to see Conservatives becoming really indignant about Conservative scandals, Liberals becoming really indignant about Liberal scandals, Socialists becoming really indignant about Socialist scandals. As it is, indignation is usually merely a form of sectarian excitement It is always easy to find something about which to become indignant in your political opponent, if it is only his good temper. His crime of crimes is that he is your political opponent—you use his minor crimes merely as rods to punish him for that. Our indignation against our opponents, to say truth, is usually ready long before the happy excuse comes which looses it like a wild beast into the arena. One sees a good example of this leashed indignation in the Ulster Unionist attitude to Nationalist Ireland. There is a silly scuffle about flags at Castledawson between a Sunday-school excursion party and a Hibernian procession, both of which ought to have known better. Not a woman or child is injured, according to the verdict of a judge on the bench, but the Ulster Unionists, armed to the teeth with indignation in advance, denounce the affair as though it were on the same level of villainy with the September Massacres. Not long afterwards real outrages break out in Belfast, and Catholics and Socialists are kicked and beaten within an inch of their lives. Here was a test of the reality of the indignation against outrages on human beings. Did the Ulstermen then come forward in a righteous fury against the wrongdoers on their own side? Not a bit of it. Sir Edward Carson did disown them in the House of Commons. But the Ulster Unionists, as a whole, raised not a breath of indignation. Being average human beings, indeed, they invariably retort to any charges made against them with an angry *tu quoque* to the South. It is not long, for instance, since a Special Commission sat to investigate the facts about sweated women workers in Belfast, and issued a report in which the prevalence of sweating was demonstrated beyond the doubt of any but a blind man. Instead, however, of directing their indignation against the evils of a system in their own midst, the Ulster Unionists—at least, one of their organs in the Press—straightway sent one of their representatives down into the South of Ireland to prove how bad wages and conditions of life were there. What a waste of indignation all this was! Munster was full of indignation against the disease of sweating in Belfast, which it could not cure. Ulster, on the other hand, was full of indignation against the disease of bad housing in Dublin, which it could not cure. There is a flavour of hypocrisy in much of this anger against sins that are outside the circle of one's own responsibility. I do not mind how many sins a man is angry with provided they include the sins he is addicted to himself and that are at his own door. There is little credit in a rich manufacturer's indignation against the evils of the land system if he is indifferent to the evils of the factory system, and landlords who denounce industrial evils but see nothing that needs redressing in the lot of the agricultural labourer are in the same boat. Perhaps, in the end, the world is served even by this outside virtue. The landlords, in order to distract attention from their own case, have more than once brought a useful indignation to bear on the case of the manufacturers, and *vice versa*, and ultimately the bewildered, ox-like public has begun to drink in a little of the truth. On the other hand, this is an unhealthy atmosphere for public virtue. It gives rise to cynical views such as are expressed in the proverb, "When thieves fall out, honest men come by their own," and in the lines concerning those who

> Compound for sins they are inclined to
> By damning those they have no mind to.

We all do it, unfortunately. The Presbyterian speaks with horror of the way in which the Catholic breaks the Sabbath, and the Catholic thinks it a terrible thing that the Presbyterian should go to a theatre on Good Friday. Montaigne, who was by inclination a sensualist, looked with disgust on the man who drank too much, and the drunkard retorts that every vice except his own is selfish and anti-social. Even when we admit our own sins we are half in love with them. It seems a less intolerable crime in oneself to rob the poor-box than in one's neighbour to have an unwashed neck. Englishmen never began to sing the praises of cleanliness as the virtue that makes a nation great until they had themselves taken to the bath. True, they often wash, as they govern themselves, not directly but by proxy; but, even so, cleanliness has been exalted into a national virtue till the very people of the slums, where the bath is used only for the storage of coal, have learned to shout "Dirty foreigner!" as the most indignant thing that can be said at a crisis.

There is nothing that makes us feel so good as the idea that some one else is an evildoer. Our scandal about our neighbours is nearly all a muttered tribute to our own virtue. It fills us with a new pride in ourselves that it was not we who gambled with trust money or made love to our neighbour's wife or ran away in battle. By kicking our neighbours down for their sins we secure for ourselves, it seems, a better place on the ladder. The object of all religion is to destroy this self-satisfied indignation with our neighbours—to make us feel that we ourselves are no better than the prostitute or the foreigner. Similarly philosophy bids us know ourselves instead of following the line of least resistance and damning others. That is why one would like to see Englishmen concerned about injuries done to Englishmen by Englishmen, even more than about injuries done to Englishmen by foreigners. Indignation against the latter, necessary though it may be, is apt to become a mere melodramatic substitute for native virtue. There are crimes enough at home for any Englishman to practise his indignation upon without ever letting his eye wander further than Dover—crimes of underpayment, crimes of overwork, crimes of rotten houses, crimes that are murder in everything but swiftness and theft in everything except illegality. It is fine, no doubt, that Englishmen should become hot with anger at the news of a Benton murdered in Mexico as it is fine that the democracies of Europe should be inflamed with indignation at the murder of a Ferrer in Spain. These things are evidence of large brotherhoods, of an extension of those family charities which are at the back of all advance in civilisation. On the other hand, can none of this passionate fraternity be spared for John Smith, aged fourteen, done to death by the half-time system, or for his father killed on the line as the result of the need of making dividends for railway shareholders, or for his mother working for a halfpenny an hour in a narrow room the filth of which is transmuted into gold for some rich man? These, too, are your brothers and sisters, and deserve the angry eloquence of an epitaph. Here is subject enough for indignation—not a weak and ineffectual indignation against foreigners, but indignation knocking terribly at your own doors.

XV
THE HEART OF MR GALSWORTHY

Mr Galsworthy has been writing to the *Times* on "the heartlessness of Parliament." The *Times*, always noted for its passion for humane causes, ranges itself behind him and asserts that Englishmen have now learned to speak of the politician "with intellectual contempt, as of one who is making a game of realities, who fiddles a dull tune while Rome is burning." Both Mr Galsworthy and the *Times* are apparently agreed that the measures which Parliament has for some time past been discussing are matters of trivial significance and, in so far as they take up time which might be devoted to better things, are an outrage upon the conscience of (to use the odd phrase of the newspaper) "those who are most interested in the spectacle of life and the future of mankind." Mr Galsworthy, wearing his heart in his inkpot not only denounces the indifference of politicians to vital things, but goes on to lay down an alternative programme—a programme of the heart, as he might call it, in contrast to the programme of the hustings. He begins his list of things which ought to be legislated about with the sweating of women workers and insufficient feeding of children, and he ends it with live instances of—in an even odder phrase than that quoted from the *Times*—"abhorrent things done daily, daily left undone."

> Export of horses worn-out in work for Englishmen—save the mark! Export that for a few pieces of blood-money delivers up old and faithful servants to wretchedness.
>
> Mutilation of horses by docking, so that they suffer, offend the eye, and are defenceless against the attacks of flies that would drive men, so treated, crazy.
>
> Caging of wild things, especially wild song-birds, by those who themselves think liberty the breath of life, the jewel above price.
>
> Slaughter for food of millions of creatures every year by obsolete methods that none but the interested defend.
>
> Importation of the plumes of ruthlessly slain wild birds, mothers with young in the nest, to decorate our gentlewomen.

Probably ninety-nine readers out of a hundred will sympathise with Mr Galsworthy's bitter cry against a Parliament that has so long left these and other wrongs unrighted. Let Mr Galsworthy take any one of his cases of inhumanity by itself, and he is sure of the support of nearly all decent people in demanding that an end shall be put to it. The human conscience has developed considerably in recent years in regard to the treatment both of human beings and of animals, and, though conscience is frequently dumb in the impressive presence of economic interests, it has still the power to get things done, as witness, for example, the establishment of minimum-wage boards in certain sweated trades. Mr Galsworthy, however, does not ask you to consider each of his desired reforms on its merits. He asks you, in effect, to put them in place of the reforms which politicians are at present discussing. "Almost any one of them," he declares of his brood of evils, "is productive of more suffering to innocent and helpless creatures, human or not, and probably of more secret harm to our spiritual life, more damage to human nature, than, for example, the admission or rejection of Tariff Reform, the Disestablishment or preservation of the Welsh Church, I would almost say than the granting or non-granting of Home Rule."

It seems to me that Mr Galsworthy is doing his cause, or causes, no service in making comparisons of this sort. He is like a man who would go before Parliament, when it was discussing some big project like the nationalisation of the railways and deny its right to legislate on such a matter till it had passed a measure forbidding the sticky sort of fly-papers. One might sympathise heartily with his desire to abolish the slow torture of flies, and I for one detest with my whole soul those filthy fly-traps in which the insects go dragging their legs out till they die. But it is obvious that the question of cruelty to flies is one which must be dealt with on its merits. To weigh it in the balance against such a thing as nationalisation of the railways is merely to invite a humorous rather than a serious treatment of the question. It is not a comic question in itself: it may easily become comic as a result of some ridiculous comparison. That is, more or less, what one feels in regard to Mr Galsworthy's implied comparison between the importance of Free Trade and the importance of putting an end to the "export of horses worn-out in work for Englishmen—save the mark! Export that for a few pieces of blood-money delivers up old and faithful servants to wretchedness." In so far as the export of horses leads to cruelty and wretchedness I agree with Mr Galsworthy that it ought to be stopped. Not because the horses are "worn out in work for Englishmen," not because they are "old and faithful servants"—that is mere sentimentalising and rhetoric—but because they are living creatures which ought not to be subjected to any pain that is not necessary. On the other hand, is not Mr Galsworthy rather unimaginative in failing to see that Tariff Reform might conceivably lead in present circumstances to intense pain and distress in every town and county in England? The imposition or non-imposition of a tariff may seem, at a superficial glance, to belong to the mere pedantry of politics. But consider the human consequences of such a thing. Every penny taken out of the pockets of the poor owing to an increase in the price of goods means the disappearance of a potential pennyworth of food from the poor man's home. Obviously, in a country where hundreds of thousands of people are living on the edge of starvation—and over it—even a slight rise in the cost of things might produce the most calamitous results. Starvation and disease and the anguish of those who have to watch their children suffer, an increase in crime and insanity and wretchedness—these are all quite conceivable results of a sudden change in the poor man's capacity to buy the necessaries of life. That is the humane Free Trader's case for Free Trade. The humane Tariff Reformer's case for Tariff Reform, on the other hand, is that a change in the fiscal system would increase wages and employment and quickly put an end to the present abominations of starvation, sweating, and unemployment. I am not concerned for the moment with the comparative merits of Free Trade and Tariff Reform. I am concerned merely with pointing out that Mr Galsworthy's theory that such a thing as the export of worn-out horses causes "more suffering to innocent and helpless creatures" than would be caused by an error in fiscal policy, affecting millions of men and women and children, does not bear a moment's examination.

Take, again, Mr Galsworthy's comparison of the case of the Home Rule Bill with the case of the caging of wild song-birds. Is not Mr Galsworthy in this instance also lacking in imagination? Had he read Irish history he would have learned a little about the "suffering to innocent and helpless creatures" that logically flows from the denial of a country's right to self-government. I will give the classic example. In the late forties of the nineteenth century, the Irish potato crop failed. The crops of corn were abundant, cattle were abundant, but the potatoes everywhere rotted in the fields under a mysterious blight. As the potato was the staple food of the people, this would have been sufficiently disastrous, even in a self-governed country. But, if Ireland had had self-government in 1847, does any one believe that her Ministers would have allowed corn and cattle to go on being exported from the country while the people were starving? Right through the Famine Ireland went on exporting grain and cattle to the value of seventeen million pounds a year so that rents might be paid. Many leading Irishmen urged the Government to pass a temporary measure prohibiting the export of foodstuffs from Ireland while the Famine lasted. This step had been taken by the Governments of Belgium and Portugal in similar circumstances. Had it been taken in Ireland—as it is incredible that it would not if the Union had not been in existence—between half a million and a million men, women, and children would have been saved from the torture of death by starvation and typhus fever. Not only this, but does not Mr Galsworthy also overlook those multiplied agonies of exile, eviction, and agrarian crime, which living creatures in Ireland would have been spared—in great measure, at least—if the country had possessed self-government? It may be doubted, whether all the wild song-birds that have ever existed since the Garden of Eden have endured among them such an excess of misery as fell to the lot of the Irish people in the half century following the Famine—much of it preventable by a simple change in the machinery of the constitution. Nor can one easily measure the amount of suffering in England indirectly due to the fact that the political intellect of the country was so occupied with the Irish question that it had not the time or the energy left to tackle scores of pressing English questions. Housing, poor law reform, half-time—these and a host of other matters have been thrust out of the way till statesmen, released from the woes of Ireland, might have time to consider them. Many Socialists have a way of forgetting the social meaning of constitutional changes. They regard constitutional reform as something that delays social reform, whereas it may be something that enables the public, if it so desires, to speed up social reform. That is why Home Rule, the abolition of the veto of the House of Lords, and a dozen comparable matters, must be as eagerly ensued by Socialists as by Radicals. The underfed child, the sweated woman—even the maltreated animal, I imagine—will benefit as a result of changes which, to say the least, take some of the impediments out of the way of the social reformer. Meanwhile, let Mr Galsworthy and those who think with him redouble their efforts on behalf of humanity, whether towards man or beast. But let them not seek to destroy a good thing that is being done in order to call attention to a good thing that is not being done. Let them not try to persuade us that it is more important for the Russian people to abolish mouse traps than to get a constitutional monarch and sound Parliamentary institutions. I have the sincerest respect for Mr Galsworthy's heart—for the generous passion with which he stands up for all the lame dogs in the world. I agree heartily with every separate cause he advocates in his letter to the *Times*. It is only his table of values with which I quarrel, and the destructive use he makes of it. I believe that an overwhelming case could be made out against Parliament on the score of its heartlessness, but Mr Galsworthy has not made it.

XVI
SPRING FASHIONS

In spite of the progress of civilisation, there are still women to whom the returning Spring is mainly a festival of dresses. It is pleasant to know that there is, after all, a remnant of primitive humanity surviving. Women will before long be the only savages. Long after the last anthropologist has departed from the last South Sea Island in despair, when the people have all become Christians and have no manners and customs left, the race of fashionable women will still march its feathered regiments up and down under the sun, a puzzle and an exasperation to the scientific inquirer. Like all really primitive people, women will go on refusing to believe in or bow down to the laws of Nature. Nature may tell them, for instance, of the correct position of the human waist; but they will not listen to her; they will insist that the human waist may be anywhere you like between the neck and the knees, according to the fashion of the moment, and Nature may as well put her fingers in her ears and go home. Savages, we are told, do not even believe in the manifest generalisation of death: they regard each new death as an entirely surprising event, due not to natural, but to accidental causes. Similarly, the fashionable woman regards the body each Spring as an entirely new body, subject to none of the generalisations which seemed appropriate to the body of even a year before. This is the grand proof she offers us of her superiority to the animals. She will have no commerce with the monotony of their ways. She will not submit herself to the regular gait of the sheep, the horse, or the cow, which is the same this year as it was in the year of Waterloo, or, for that matter, in the year of Salamis. She claims for her body the liberty to move one year with the long stride of a running fowl, and the next at a hobble like a spancelled goat. It might be said of her that she is not one animal, but all the animals. She will borrow from all Nature, dead and alive, indeed, as greedily as a poet. She will colour her hair to look like a gorse-bush and her lips to look like a sunset. She will capture the green from the grass, the purple from the hills, the blue from Eastern seas, the silver from the mists, as it suits her fancy. One year she will demand of life that it shall be gorgeous in hue as a baboon's courtships; the next, that it shall be as colourless as a rook's funeral. She enters upon the labour of life as though it were a long series of disguises. Probably it was her success in passing from form to form that led the ancient Greeks to suspect the presence of nymphs now in trees, now in running water, and now even in the hills. Everywhere in Nature man sees evasive woman. There is nothing anywhere, from a mountain valley in flower to a chestnut tree glistening into bud, which does not remind him of something about her—her hats, her cloaks, or her ribbons. Such a plunderer of beauties would, one cannot but feel, become a great artist if only she possessed some standards. But she dresses without standards, without philosophy: there is nothing but appetite in it all, and a capricious appetite at that. She has no settled principle but the principle of change. She flies from grace to ugliness lightheartedly, indiscriminately. She is like the kind of butterfly which you could get only in a fairy tale—a butterfly that could change itself into a mouse, and from a mouse into a dandelion, and from a dandelion into a camel, and from a camel into a grasshopper, and from a grasshopper into a cat, and so on through a thousand transformations. Her world leaves us giddy like the transformation scene in a pantomime. In her artistic ideals she is a follower, not of Orpheus, but of Proteus.

Yet who can disparage her April ritual? She is in league with the whole singing earth, which once a year sets out on its long procession of praise. Her new fashions are but an item in the general rejoicing over the infinite resurrections of Nature. Every thorn-bush gowns itself in green, a ghost of beauty. Every laurel puts forth new leaves like little green flames. There is a glow in the grass as though some spirit lurked behind it deeper a million times than its roots. Everywhere Nature has relit the sacred fire. She has given us back warmth—the warmth in which food increases and birds sing; and we can no more escape her gladness than if we had been rescued from the perils and privations of a siege. This is the time when men wake up to find they are alive, and their exultation makes them poets. One of the first things of which man seems to have become conscious in the world about him was the renewal of life each spring.

> The earth does like a snake renew
> Her winter weeds outworn.

Once a year he beheld the coming of the golden age again. He worshipped the serpent as the emblem of endless life long before he learned to suspect it as the devil. He may have been an infidel as he shivered in the winter rains, but the lark leaping into the sun awakened the old splendid credulity again. He knows that Persephone will rise. Hence the divine madness that possesses him year by year at this season—a madness which nowadays expresses itself largely in throwing hard balls at coconuts. Possibly this symbolises the contemptuous smashing of the winter's fears, for is there anything which looks more like a withered fear than one of those grisly brown bearded fruits? And do not the showman's cries and his bell-ringings at the coconut saloon make up a clamour like the clamour of the savage beating forth the flock of his superannuated terrors? He is the incarnation of the boastful faith that has returned to us. Perhaps, too, the coconuts may be symbols of the hoarded food supply of the winter—the supply which we were continually in dread might come to a slow close, and which we can now rail at and insult in our revived confidence in the green world.

Certainly this enthusiasm of ours for the spring is not all so disinterested as it appears. We are hungry animals before we are poetical animals, and we are often praising the promise of our food when we seem to be most exalted in our raptures. It may be that even the pleasure we take in the singing of birds is simply a relic of the pleasure which primitive man felt as he heard the voice of many dinners making its way back to him at the turn of the year. But the appeal of music and colour need not be so detailedly stomachic as that. Man may not have loved the lark's song because he wanted in particular to eat the lark, or, indeed, any bird. He may have loved it merely as a significant voice amid the chorus and banners of the returning hosts of eatable things. If it were not so, many of our tastes would be different. Among the smells and colours of spring those we love most are not the smells and colours of eatable things, but of inculinary things, like roses, and if we loved the music of birds by some standard of the stomach, it is the crowing of the cock and not the song of the lark that would inspire us to poetry. It is the grunting of the pig and not the cuckoo's call which would startle in us the thrill of romance.

There is, on the other hand, just a chance that natural man does respond more sympathetically to the voice of the cock and the pig than to the speech of the cuckoo and the skylark. The difference between the farmer's and the artist's taste in landscape is proverbial. When man looks at the world and sums it up in terms of food, he is indifferent to masses of colour and runs of music. His favourite colour is the colour of a good crop of corn or a field of grass that will fatten the cattle. He cares less for silver streams than for the drains in his turnip-fields. Whether the love of the more ornamental things— the useless songs of the birds and the scent of flowers, which is a prosaic thing only to the bees—is an advance on this passion for utility may be questioned by the advocates of the simple life. Ornament, they may contend, especially in woman's dress, is simply mannikin's vainglory. Woman was first hung or robed with precious things, not in order that she might be happy, but in order that man might be able to boast of her among his neighbours. She was as sure a sign of his power as a string of enemies' heads hanging from his waist. She was the advertisement of his riches. Before long woman became happy in her golden slavery. Wisely so, perhaps, for in the end she was able to make use of the man's fatuous love of boasting to exact high terms for aiding him in his conspiracy of magnificence. She studied the science of surprise, and applied it to the labour of dressing herself in such a way as to make him slavishly regard her as the most wonderful being on earth. If we may trust the testimony of Mrs Edith Wharton's novels, woman has so subjugated man with this chameleon brilliance of hers in modern America that he thinks himself quite happy if she makes use of him as the hodman of her charms. Thus in the spring fashions we may see the triumph of a sex rather than a hymn of colour to the revival of Nature. It is a lamentable declension in theory, and therefore I do not entirely believe it. I still hold to the conviction that the gaiety of women's Easter dress is in some manner allied to the gaiety of the earth. It is but a decrepit gaiety compared to what it might be. But that is because of its long association with all sorts of alien things — the necessity of the man — hunt, the pride of the church parade, and the rest of it. When woman meets man on equal terms she will, one hopes in one's credulous moments, cultivate beauty more and fashion less. She will no longer be estranged from the morning stars that sing together and the little hills that clap their hands. Her feet will be beautiful in Bond Street, and Regent Street shall have cause to shout for joy.

XVII
ON BLACK CATS

It is easy to imagine the enthusiasm of the audience at Manchester when a black cat walked on to the platform at a meeting of Sir Edward Carson's. Lord Derby, who presided, hailed it as an omen of the success of the Ulster cause. He went on to tell the audience that the last Unionist victory in Manchester had been presaged by the appearance of a black cat in some polling booth or other. That, you may be sure, was the most convincing argument in the night's speech-making. People who will stumble over the logic of politics for a lifetime can appreciate the logic of the black cat in a fraction of a second. Black cats, indeed, are one of the very few things in which a good many unbelievers nowadays believe. These are the substitute for the angels and devils of our grandfathers. We are sceptics in everything but our superstitions. The most superstitious people of all are often to be found among those who do not believe in God, and who would not dream of entering a church-gate unless there was no other way of avoiding walking under a ladder. These it is who pick up pins with the greatest enthusiasm, and who become downcast if a dog howls, and who had rather not sleep at all than sleep in a room numbered thirteen. They will deride the cherubim and the seraphim, but they will not risk offending the demon to whom they throw an oblation of the salt they have just spilt on the table. It is as though each man carried his own little firmament of immortals about with him, and sacrificed to them on his own infinitesimal altars. This is not, I suspect, because he loves them, but because he fears them. He regards them as a species of blackmailers—the Scottish way of looking at fairies. Nearly every portent is to him a portent of misfortune. The number thirteen, the spilling of salt, the bay of a dog, the sight of a red-haired man first thing on New Year's morning, dreams about babies—these things cast a gloom over his world deeper than midnight; and of this kind are nearly all the portents which wriggle like little snakes in the superstitious imagination.

It is the distinction of the black cat that he is one of the few cheerful superstitions left to us. Why he should be so no one can tell us, and he has not been considered so in all times or in all places. He has even been regarded on occasion as the false shape of a witch. Perhaps, the origin of all our care of him was the tenderness of fear. He may be like the black god worshipped by the ancient Slavs who were indifferent to his white brother-god. They did this, we are told, because they thought that the white god was so good that they had nothing to fear from him in any case. But the black god one could not trust, and so one had to buy his goodwill. It seems not improbable that the veneration of the black cat may have begun in much the same way. The smile with which our ancestors first greeted him was, I fancy, a nervous, doubting smile, like the smile with which many of us try to cajole snarling dogs. Then, gradually, as he did not leap upon them and destroy them, they came to believe less and less in his will to do evil, and in the end he was canonised, and now he has been accepted as a sound English Tory, which is generally admitted to be the highest type of animal that Nature has produced.

Two centuries or so ago Addison poured such finished contempt on all superstitions of this kind that it would have been difficult to believe that men and women of intellect would still be clinging to them to-day. At the same time, their survival is the most natural thing in the world. They are bound to survive in a world in which men live not in faiths and enjoyments, but in hopes and fears. Faith is the way of religion, and enjoyment is the way of philosophy; but hopes and fears are the coloured lights that illuminate the exciting way of superstition. If we are creatures of hopes and fears we have no sun, and our lights have a trick of appearing and disappearing like will-o'-the-wisps, leading us a pretty dance whither we know not. Every step we take we expect to unfold the secret. We find omens in the direction of straws, in the running of hares, in the flight of birds. If the girl of hopes and fears wishes to know what colour of a man she is going to marry, she waits till she hears the cuckoo in summer, and then examines the sole of her shoe in the expectation of finding a hair on it which will be the colour of her future husband's head. I will make a confession of my own. I have never listened slavishly for the cuckoo, but many years ago I had as foolish a superstition about farthings. I believed that they were luck-bringers. At the time I was lodging in the traditional garret in Pimlico, trying more or less vainly to make a living by writing. Whenever I had sent off a manuscript I used to go out the same evening to a little shop where, when they sold a loaf, they always gave you a farthing change out of your threepence. How cheerily I used to leave the shop with the loaf under my arm and the farthing in my pocket! That farthing, I felt, could be trusted to cast a spell on the editor towards whom the manuscript was flying. It would be as effective as an introduction from one of the crowned heads of Europe. And even if, a night or two afterwards, the most loathsome of all visible objects—a returned manuscript—made the lodging-house look still more sordid than before, I abated no jot of my trust. My heart sank for the moment, but in the end I settled down to acceptance of the fact that there was a fool sitting in an editor's chair who could resist even the power of farthings. On the next day, or the day after, I would set out with revived hope for the baker's shop again. I remember the acute misery I felt on one occasion when I went into a more pretentious shop, where the girl put my loaf in the scales and asked me whether I would prefer a small roll or a part of a loaf to make up the full threepenceworth of weight. I would have given my boots, and even my old hat, to be able to say, "Please, may I have my farthing?" But my courage failed. There are things one cannot say to a pretty shop-girl. Years afterwards I happened to be discussing superstitions with a friend, and I instanced the well-known belief in the luckiness of farthings. "But farthings aren't supposed to be lucky," said my friend, with a smile of authority: "they're supposed to be extremely unlucky." It was as though the world reeled. Here I had been steadily building up ruin for myself all that time with my miser's hoard of farthings. I felt like the man in *The Silver King* who cries: "Turn back, O wheels of the Universe, and give me back my yesterday!" If only I could get back some of my yesterdays, I would assuredly buy my bread in that big, bright shop where the girl gives you full weight for your threepence; and never would I set foot in that little low shop where a half-blind old man wraps your loaf in a page of newspaper, and lays in your hand a dirty farthing that is only the price of your undoing.

It is, perhaps, natural that my experience should have left me rather unfriendly to superstitions. I cannot believe that the universe, or even a single planet of it, is ruled by imps of chance which express themselves in the doings of crows, and in floating tea-leaves and in the dropping of umbrellas. Better join the church of the Sea-Dyaks of Borneo, if one can find nothing better to believe in than that. It is in order to protest against the heathen religion of crows and numbers and tea-leaves that I sometimes deliberately leap on to a 'bus numbered thirteen, or walk under a ladder rather than go round it. Occasionally, I say, for my mood varies. There are days when I feel like turning a blind eye to 'bus number 13, and when a crow, sitting and cawing on the roof of the church opposite, gives me the shivers. It is in vain that I tell myself that the last superstition is the most irrational of all, because in some places the sight of one crow is supposed to be lucky, the sight of two unlucky, while in other places the reverse is the case, and apart from this, the superstition does not refer to crows at all, but to magpies. Then, again, when I am arguing against the dislike of setting out on a Friday, I find myself compelled to admit that the holiday in which I was not able to get away till Saturday was, on the whole, the best I ever had. But the salt—I refuse to throw salt over my shoulder, no matter what happens. I prefer to exorcise the demon with some formula from trigonometry, as I once heard a man doing when he passed under a ladder. And if I retain a hankering faith in black cats, it is, as I have said, the most cheerful superstition in the world. About two months ago I was sitting one night in the depths of gloom expecting news of a tragedy. Suddenly, I heard a cat mewing as if in difficulties. It seemed some way up the road, and I thought that it must be caught in a hedge, or that somebody was tormenting it. I went downstairs and put my hat on to go out and look for it, and had hardly opened the door, when in walked a little black kitten with bright eyes and its tail in the air. I defy anyone to have disbelieved in black kittens at that moment. It seemed more like an omen than anything I have ever known. I had never seen the kitten before, and its owner has reclaimed it since. But I cannot help being grateful to it for anticipating with its gleaming eyes the happy news that reached me a day or two later. Of course, I do not believe the black cat superstition any more than I believe that it is unlucky to see the new moon for the first time through glass. But still, if you happen to be requiring a black cat at any time, I advise you to make quite sure that there are no white hairs in its coat. One white hair spoils all, and puts it on a level with any common squaller in the back garden.

XVIII
ON BEING SHOCKED

Being shocked is evidently still one of the favourite pastimes of the British people. There has been something of a festival of it since the production of Mr Shaw's new play. Even the open Bible, it appears, is not a greater danger to souls than *Androcles and the Lion*. Of course, the open Bible has become generally accepted in England now, but one remembers how the Church used to censor it, and one looks back to the first men who protested against its being banned as to bright heroes of adventure. Everybody knows, however, that if the Bible were not already an accepted book—if we could read it with a fresh eye as a book written by real people like ourselves and only just published for the first time—it would leave most of us as profoundly shocked as Canon Hensley Henson, who, though he does not want to limit its circulation, is eager at least to expurgate it for the reading of simple persons. I do not, I may say, quarrel with Canon Henson. Every man has a right to be shocked so long as it is his own shock and not a mere imitation of somebody else's. What one has no patience with is the case of those people who are always shocked in herds. They are intellectually too lazy to be shocked, so to say, off their own bat. So they join a mob of the shocked as they might join a demonstration in the streets or a political party. They are so lacking in initiative that, instead of boldly being shocked themselves, they frequently even are content to be shocked by proxy. In the world of the theatre they hire the Censor to be shocked for them by all the immoral plays that are written. The Censor having been duly shocked, the public feels that it has done all that can be expected of it in that direction and it refuses to turn a hair afterwards no matter what it sees in the theatre. It takes schoolgirls to musical comedies which are as often as not mere tinkling farces of lust. But it does not care. It has handed over its capacity for being shocked to the Censor, and nothing can stir it out of the happy sleep of its faculties any more—nothing, I should add, except a Shaw play. For even the chalk of a dozen censors could not remove the offence of Mr Shaw. He is like an evangelist who would suddenly rise up at a garden party and talk about God. He is as bad form as one of those enthusiastic converts who corner us in railway trains or buttonhole us in the streets to ask us if we are saved. He is a Salvationist who has broken into the playhouse, and, as he unfolds the knockabout comedy of redemption, we are aware that we no longer feel knowing and superior, as we expect the winking laughter of the theatre to make us feel, but ignorant and simple, like a child singing its first hymns. That is the mood, at any rate, of *Androcles and the Lion*. That is the offence and the stone of stumbling. Mr Shaw has stripped some of our most sacred feelings as bare as babies, and we do not know what to do to express our sense of the indecency.

It is clear, then, that being shocked is simply a way of recovering our balance. It is also a way of recovering our sense of superiority. There is more pleasure in being shocked by the sin of one's neighbour or one's neighbour's wife than in eating cream buns. Not, indeed, that it is always the sins that shock us most. Much as we enjoy the whisper of how a great man beats his wife, or a poet drinks, or some merry Greek has flirted her virtue away, we would shake our heads over them with equal gravity if they had the virtues of Buddhist monks and sisters. It is the virtues that shock us no less than the vices. Perhaps it was because Swinburne gave utterance to the horror a great many quite normal people feel for virtue that, in spite of an intellect of far from splendid quality, he ended his life as something of a prophet. Tolstoi never shocked Europe more than a hair's weight so long as he blundered through the seven sins like nearly any other man of his class. He only scandalised us when he began to try to live in literal obedience to the Sermon on the Mount. When we are in church, no doubt, we say fie to the young man who had great possessions and would not sell all that he had and give to the poor, as Jesus commanded him. But in real life we should be troubled only if the young man took such a command seriously. Obviously, then, the psychology of being shocked cannot be explained in terms of triumphant virtue. We must look for an explanation rather in the widespread instinct which forbids a man to be different either in virtues or in vices from other people. It arises out of a loyalty to ordinary standards, which the average man has made for his comfort—perhaps, we should say, for his self-respect. To deny these standards in one's life is like denying a foot-rule—which would be an outrage on the common-sense of the whole trade union of carpenters. Or one might put it this way. To live publicly like a saint is as disturbing as if you were to ask a tailor to measure your soul instead of your legs. It is to whisk your neighbour into a world of new dimensions—to leave him dangling where he can scarcely breathe. This does not, it may be thought, explain the attitude of the shocked man towards sinners. But, after all, we are very tolerant of sinners until they break some code of our class. John Bright defended adulteration because he was a manufacturer. Grocers object to the forgery of cheques, which is a danger to their business, in a manner in which they do not object to the forgery of jam, which puts money in their purses. We are more shocked by the man who gets drunk furiously once in six months than by the man who tipples all the time, not because the former is more surely destroying himself, but because he is more likely to do something that will inconvenience business or society. We can forgive almost all sins except those that inconvenience us. There are others, it may be argued, that we hate for their own sake. But is not a part of our hatred even of these due to the fact that they inconvenience our minds, having about them something novel or immeasurable? It is in the last analysis that breaches of codes and conventions shock us most. If your uncle danced down Piccadilly dressed like a Chinaman, your sense of propriety would be more outraged than if he appeared in the Divorce Court, since, bad as the latter is, it is less bewilderingly abnormal. Mr Wells, in *The Passionate Friends*, offers a defence of the conventions by which Society attempts to reduce us all to a common pattern. He sees in them, as it were, angels with flaming swords against the remorseless individualism that flesh is heir to. They are a sort of compulsion to brotherhood. They are signs to us that we must not live merely to ourselves, but that we must in some way identify ourselves with the larger self of human society. It is a tempting paradox, and, in so far as it is true, it is a defence of all the orthodoxies that have ever existed. Every orthodoxy is a little brotherhood of men. At least, it is so until it becomes a little brotherhood of parrots. It only breaks down when some horribly original person discovers the old truth that it is a shocking thing for men to be turned into parrots, and gives up his life to the work of rescuing us from our unnatural cages. Perhaps a brotherhood of parrots is better than no brotherhood at all. But the worst of it is, the conventions do not gather us into one brood even of this kind. They sort us into a thousand different painted and chattering groups, each screaming against the other like, in the vulgar phrase, the Devil. No: brotherhood does not lie that way. Perched vainly in his cage of malice and uncharitableness, man feels more like a boss than a brother. There is nothing so like an average superman as a parrot.

The passion for being shocked, then, must be redeemed from its present cheapness if it is to help us on the way to being fit for the double life of the individual and society. We must learn to be shocked by the normal things—by the conventions themselves rather than by breaches of the conventions. Those who lift their hands in pious horror over conventional Christianity should also lift their hands in pious horror over conventional un-Christianity. The conventions are often merely truths that have got the sleeping-sickness; but by this very fact they are disabled as regards any useful purpose. Every great leader, whether in religion or in the reform of society, comes to us with living truths to take the place of conventions. He gives the lie to our bread-and-butter existence, and teaches us to be shocked by most things to which we are accustomed and many things which we have treasured. Society progresses only in so far as it learns to be shocked, not by other people, but by itself. What did England ever gain except a purr or a glow from being shocked by French morals or German manners? The English taste for being shocked is only worth its weight in old iron when it is directed on some thing such as the procession of the poor and the ill-clad that circulates from morning till night in the streets of English slums. Being shocked is a maker of revolutions and literatures when men are shocked by the right things—or, rather, by the wrong things. Out of a mood of shock came Blake's fiery rout of proverbs in that poem which begins:

> A Robin Redbreast in a cage
> Puts all heaven in a rage.

It is, unfortunately, not the Robin Redbreast in a cage that shocks us most now. It is rather the Robin Redbreast which revolts against being expected to sit behind bars and sing like a mechanical toy. Our resurrection as men and women will begin when we learn to be shocked by our mechanical servitudes, as Ruskin and Morris used to be in their fantastic way, instead of being shocked, as we are at present—the conventionally good, the conventionally bad, and the conventionally artistic who are too pallid to be either—by what are really only our immortal souls. At our present stage of evolution, Heaven would shock us far more than earth has succeeded in doing. That is at once our condemnation and our comedy.

XIX
CONFESSIONS

Father Hugh Benson has been praised for his courage in confessing that he could not read Sir Walter Scott. Surely this must be a world of lies if it is remarkable to find a man honest in so simple a matter as his tastes in literature. All but one—or it may even be a few hundred—we are under the empire of shame, which withers truth upon our lips and threatens us with the rack if we do not confess things that are lies. That is the reason why in any given year we all appear to have the same tastes. This year it is Croce; last year it was Bergson; the year before that it was William James; the year before that it was Nietzsche. In advanced circles you can already say what you like about Bergson. You will hardly dare to be frank about Croce till after midsummer. It is the same in literature as in philosophy. Twenty years ago we were all swearing that Stevenson and Kipling were two such artists as England had never seen before. We did not say they were greater than Dickens and Shakespeare. We simply accepted them as incomparable. To-day, no one who is not middle-aged speaks of Mr Kipling as an artist, and one is humoured as a fogey by boys and girls if one mentions Stevenson seriously in a discussion on literature. Nor can we blame this popular changeableness as entirely dishonest. We may love an author for his novelty for a time, as we loved Swinburne for his novel metres and Mr Kipling for his novel brutalities; and after a while, when the novelty has faded, we may see that there is little enough left—too little, at any rate, to justify our primrose praises. It is an ignominious confession to make that we have been taken in by a new kind of powder and paint, but, as everybody else has been taken in and afterwards disillusioned in the same way and in the same hour, that does not trouble us. We do not mind being ignominious in regiments. It is the refusal to right-about-face and to march at the public word of command that would be the difficult thing. We had rather go wrong with the crowd than be solitary and conspicuous in our rectitude. In the Sunday-school we used to sing "Dare to be a Daniel," but we sang it with a thousand voices. The lion's den was an acclaimed resort for the childish imagination at the moment. In one's surroundings, as a matter of fact, one could have achieved resemblance to Daniel only by some such extreme step as casting doubt upon his historical existence. Had one done so, the commiteee of the school would quickly have made it clear that Daniel in short breeches and a white Sunday tie was a most undesirable person. It has always been as great a crime to behave like Daniel as it has been an act of piety to praise him.

It is because there are so few who are willing to face the terrors of isolation that any one who will do so gains an easy notoriety. A man has only to confess quite honestly that he has individual tastes and failings in order to take a place among men of genius. His confession, however, must be as honest as if vanity and pretence had never been known. It is not enough that he should confess his vices. It may be more fashionable at the time to confess one's vices than one's virtues. When a confession is merely a form of boasting it becomes as frivolous as Dr Cook's story of his discovery of the Pole. There is a natural humility in the great books of confessions: the writers of sham-confessions are no more capable of the act of bending than a balloon. It is possible to give the life-story of every sin one has ever committed and yet to remain dishonest. One may be attitudinising even while one tells the truth. It is, it may be granted, extraordinarily difficult to see oneself truly and without bias, and to refrain from discovering excuses for oneself faster almost than one discovers one's faults. It is this humbug sense of excuses in the background that makes most of us the merest pretenders when we confess that we are blackguards, and call ourselves by other insulting names. Our confessions are as often as not mean attempts to forestall the accusations of those we have injured. We make them in the hope of turning anger into pity, and when the trick has succeeded we laugh in secret triumph over the simplicity of human nature. Anatole France has maintained that all the good writers of confessions, from Augustine onwards, are men who are still a little in love with their sins. It is a paradox with the usual grain of truth. The self-analyst, probably enough, will fall in love with the material on which he works just as the surgeon does. One has heard surgeons wax enthusiastic over some unique case of disease which they have cured. They will even speak of such things as "lovely." It is thus a fighter shakes hands with his opponent. Similarly, the saint with his sins. For him they will always be illuminated, as it were, by grace. Saints have even been known to thank God for their sins as the means of their salvation. On the other hand, no good book of confessions is mere play-acting—lip-service to heaven, secret gratitude to the devil. When confession becomes a luxury of this dramatic sort, one may begin to suspect oneself as but a refined sort of sensualist. There are moods of false exaltation in which the confession that one has broken a commandment seems to add an inch to one's stature. The true confessor, on the other hand, will as soon confess a mouse as a mountain. He will not begin, like Baudelaire in the café: "On the night I killed my father...." He will more likely tell us, like Pepys, how he beat the servant-girl with a broom, or how, like Horace, he threw away his shield and ran from the battle. Pepys lives in literature because he was unblushingly, unboastingly, frank about his littleness—his jealousy of his wife, his petty conquests of other women, his eternal sensualities mixed with his eternal prayers. How vitally he portrays himself in a thousand sentences like: "I took occasion to be angry with my wife before I rose about her putting up half-a-crown of mine in a paper box, which she had forgotten where she had lain it. But we were friends again, as we are always!" Between that and the artistic attitude of naughtiness in a book like Mr George Moore's *Memoirs of My Dead Life*, what a gulf there is! The one is as fresh a piece of nature as a thorn-tree on a hill-side; the other is as near life as the cloak-and-dagger plays of the theatre. English prose literature has suffered immensely during the last century because it has shrunk from the honesty of Mr Pepys and attitudinised, now in the manner of Prince Albert, now in the manner of Mr Moore. It has worn the white flower of a blameless life—or the opposite— instead of the white sheet of repentance. It has suffered from the obsession at one time of sex, at another time of sexlessness. It has seldom, like modern Russian literature, been the confession of a man's or a people's soul.

It is not only in literature, however, that the supreme genius is the genius of confession. One demands the same kind of honest and personal speech from one's friends. One cannot be friends with a man who is not a man but an echo. The poets have sung of echo as a beautiful thing. It may be well enough among the mountains, but who would live in a world of echoes? One demands of one's friend that he shall be himself, even though it involves a liking for the poems of Mr G. R. Sims, rather than that he should be a boneless imitation who can talk the current jargon about Picasso and the cubists. To confess that one has no taste for the latest fad in the arts and philosophy is becoming a rarer and rarer form of originality. We utter our pallid judgments in terror at once of the clique of the moment and of posterity. We are afraid that our contemporaries may tell us that we no longer can keep abreast of *les jeunes*, but are become ossified. We are afraid that our grandchildren will look back on us with the smiling superiority with which we look back on those who raved against Wagner and flung epithets at Ibsen. Be in no trouble about that. Your grandchildren will smile at you in any case. Has not the reputation of Matthew Arnold already sunk lower than that of the reviewers in the daily papers? Is not even Pater being thrust into a second grave as an indolent driveller without judgment? There is no phylactery against the poor opinion of one's grandchildren. Nor need we be greatly in fear of damning bad art because an occasional Wagner has been condemned. After all, there were other people condemned besides Wagner. They were so bad, however, that we have forgotten what the critics said about them. Pope wrote his *Dunciad* not against the Wagners and Ibsens of his day, but against all those fashionable fellows whose names survive only in his satire. No one would have the courage to write a *Dunciad* to-day. We have discovered that there are no dunces except the people who were the vogue yesterday. Thus we chorus the season's reputations. We are ready to stab last week's gods in the back if it happens to be the fashion. We can all say what we please about Shakespeare now that it no longer requires courage to do so, but we dare not confess with equal frankness our feelings about some little wren of a minor poet who came out of the shell a month ago. The world has become a maze of echoes in which no honest conversation can be heard for the dull reverberant speech of the walls.

XX
THE TERRORS OF POLITICS

There is a good deal to be said for Mr Lloyd George's complaint against the world for its treatment of politicians. In one sense, it may be better to throw a brick at a politician than to trust him. It encourages the others. Unhappily, it is a habit that, once acquired, is by no means easy to discontinue. One throws one's first brick as a public duty; before one has got through one's first cart-load, however, one is throwing for the sheer exhilaration of the thing. It is difficult, for instance, to believe that if Mr Leo Maxse went to Paradise itself, he would be able to forget his cunning with the words "swindlers," "rogues," and "cabals"; one feels sure that he would discover some angels requiring to be denounced for singing "cocoa" hymns, and some committee of the saints which it was necessary to arraign as Foozle & Co. The popularity of Mr Maxse's redundant abuse in *The National Review* seems to me to be one of the most significant phenomena of the day. It is a symptom of the reviving taste for looking on one's political opponent not only as a public, but as a private, villain. There was probably never a time when it was a more popular amusement, both in print and at the dinner table, to give a twist of criminality to the portraiture of political enemies. When Daniel O'Connell denounced Disraeli as "the heir-at-law of the blasphemous thief who died on the cross," he was abusing him, not for his home life, but as a public figure. Similarly, when Sir William Harcourt described Mr Chamberlain as "a serpent gnawing a file," he said nothing which would make even the most proper lady shrink from bowing to Mr Chamberlain in the street. The modern sort of nomenclature, however, has gone beyond this. It is a constant suggestion that Cabinets are recruited from Pentonville and Wormwood Scrubs. One would hardly be surprised, on meeting a Prime Minister nowadays, to find that he had the bristly chin and the club of Bill Sikes. As for the rank and file of Ministers, one does not insult Bill Sikes by comparing them to him. One thinks of them rather as on the level with racecourse sneak-thieves and the bullies of disorderly houses. Decidedly, they are not persons to take tea with.

Calumny, of course, is as old as Adam — or, at least, as Joseph — and one remembers that even Mr Gladstone was accused of the vulgarest immorality till a journalist tracked him down and discovered that it was rescue work, and not the deadly sin with the largest circulation, which was his private hobby. That sort of libel no man can escape who risks remaining alive. Perhaps we should come to hate our public men as the Athenians came to hate Aristides if we could find nothing evil to think about them. What the politician of the present day has to fear is not an occasional high tide of calumny, or even a volley of the old-fashioned abusive epithets, which are, so to speak, all in the day's play. It is rather the million-eyed beast of suspicion which democracies every now and then take to their bosoms as a pet. Often it seems a noble beast, for it is impossible to be suspicious all the time without sometimes suspecting the truth. Its food, however, is neither primarily truth nor primarily falsehood; it thrives on both indifferently. And one foresees that, during the transition stage between the break-up of the old manners of servility and the inauguration of the new manners of service, this beast is going to be more voracious than ever. This may from some points of view be a good thing. It will be an announcement, at least, of new forces struggling to become politically articulate. On the other hand from the politician's point of view, it will be not only deplorable, but terrifying. It will be worse than having to fight wild beasts in the arena. Politics, it is safe to prophesy, will before long call for as cool a nerve, as determined a heroism, as aviation.

It may be that things have always been like this—that base motives have been imputed to politicians ever since politics began—that one's political enemies always charged one with a dishonest greed for the spoils of office and all the rest of it. But the terror of the politics of the future is likely to be, not that one will be abused by one's enemies, but that one will be abused by one's friends. That is the tendency in a democracy which has not yet found itself. It is a tendency which one sees occasionally at work to-day at labour conventions. The unofficial leaders denounce the official leaders; the official leaders retort in kind; and the hosts of Labour set out to face the enemy tugging at each other's ears. There is no job on earth less enviable than the job of a Labour leader. The Tory and Radical leaders are supported at least in public by their respective parties; but the Labour leader at home among his followers is commonly regarded as a cross between a skunk and a whited sepulchre. As a rule, it may be, he deserves all he gets, but the point is that he would get it just the same whether he deserved it or not. The light that beats upon a Labour M.P.'s seat on the platform is a thousand times fiercer and more devouring than any that ever beat upon a throne. This partly arises from the fact that the working classes are less practised than others in concealing what passes through their minds. If they suspect the worst they say so instead of passing a vote of thanks to the object of their suspicions. Further, they are still fresh enough to politics to be very exacting in their demands upon politicians. Other people have got accustomed to the idea that lawyers, whether Liberal or Tory, do not go into the House of Commons, as the Americans say, for their health. They have settled down comfortably to regard politics as a field of personal ambition even more than a field of public service. No doubt the two aims are, to a great extent, compatible, but, even so, no one expects the ordinary party politician to have the faith that goes to the stake for a conviction. Labour, on the other hand, in so far as it is articulate, does demand faith of this kind from its leaders. If they do not possess it already it is prepared to thump it into them with a big stick.

The difficulty is to retain this faith after one has been, as it were, inside politics. One goes into politics believing in the faith that will remove mountains: one remains in politics believing in the machine that will remove mole-hills. It is only the rare politician who does not ultimately succumb to the fatal fascination of the machine. It may be the party machine or the Parliamentary machine or the administrative machine. In any case, and to whatever party he belongs, he soon comes to take it for granted, not that the machine must be made to do what the people want, but that the people must learn to be patient, even to the point of reverence, with the machine, and must be careful to keep it supplied, not with the vinegar of criticism, but with the oil of agreement, which alone enables its wheels to run smoothly. Democracy has again and again had to rise up and smash its machines, just because they had become idols in this way. No doubt, even were Socialism in full swing, the idolatry of machinery would still, to some extent, continue, and new machines would constantly have to be invented to take the place of the old as soon as the latter began to acquire this pseudo-religious sanction. There will probably still also be people who will go about wanting to destroy machinery from a rather illogical idea that anything which is even capable of being turned into an idol must be evil. The politicians and the anti-politicians will always stand to each other in the relation of priests and iconoclasts. "Priests of machinery," indeed, would be a much more realistic description of most politicians than Mr Lloyd George's phrase, "priests of humanity."

There you have the politician's doom. There you have the real terror for the good man going into politics. He dreads not that he will be called names so much as that he will deserve them. Office, he knows, is as perilous a gift as riches, and the temptation to be a tyrant, if it is only in a committee room down a side street, has destroyed men who stood out like heroes against drink and the flesh and gold. The House of Commons could easily drift into becoming the house of the six hundred tyrants, if only the public would permit it. There is no amulet against the despotism of politicians except living opinions among the people. It would be foolish, however, merely because politicians are in danger of setting themselves up as tyrants, to propose to exterminate them. They can, if taken in time and domesticated, be made at least as useful as the horse and the cow. Indeed, so long as they are content to be regarded merely as our poor brothers, they can be as useful as any other human beings almost, except the saints. But they must demand no sacrosanctity for their position. At present, when they denounce people for abusing them, they are as often as not angry merely at being criticised. They are too fond of thinking that it is the chief function of the electors to pass votes of confidence in them. That is why, heartily as I love politicians, I would keep them on a chain. But I would not throw stones at them in their misery. I would even feed the brutes.

XXI
ON DISASTERS

It is a remarkable thing that human beings have never yet got reconciled to disaster. Each new disaster, like the ship on fire, the burning mine and the wrecked train inspires us with a new horror, as though it were something without precedent. Occasionally in the history of the world horror has been heaped on horror till people became indifferent. During the Reign of Terror, for instance, the tragic death of a man or woman became so everyday an affair that before long it was regarded with almost as little emotion as a stumble on the stairs. Luckily, the periods are rare in which this terrible indifference is possible to us. It is only by keeping our sense of disaster sharp and burnished that we shall ever succeed in stirring ourselves into action against it. On the other hand, it is amazing for how brief a period the impulse to action in most of us lasts. On the morrow of a great preventable disaster it is as if the whole human race stood up with bared heads and swore in the presence of Heaven that this abominable thing should never be allowed to occur again. But, alas! a full meal and a bottle of wine do wonders in restoring the rosy view of life. Our tears which at first seemed to flow from the depths of our hearts soon give place to commonplaces of the lips and to sighs that actually increase our sense of comfort rather than otherwise. We who but yesterday realised that trusting to luck was a crime far deadlier in its effects than a mere passionate murder will to-morrow accommodate ourselves once more to the accidental medley of life which at least justified itself in letting so many of our fathers and grandfathers die in their beds.

This accommodation of ourselves to life, it is curious to reflect, is just the consenting to drift without a star which is condemned by all the religions. Life is conceived in the religions as a vigilance. If we are not vigilant, we are damned. It is the same in politics, where we all quote Burke's sentence about eternal vigilance being the price of liberty. But religion and politics do not long survive the dessert. We are as much in love with drowsiness as the lotus-eaters, and at a seemingly safe distance we are as careless of the ruin of the skies as Horace's just man. Preachers may tell us once a week that we are sentinels sleeping at our posts, and, if they say it eloquently enough, we may possibly raise their salaries. But we have got used to sleeping at our posts, and what we have got used to, we feel in our bones, cannot be regarded as a very serious sin. Once, in the fine wakefulness of our youth, we summoned the world out of its sleep. But our voices sounded so thin and lonely in the sleep-laden air that we felt rather ashamed of ourselves, and we soon climbed down out of our golden balconies and took our places with our brothers among the hosts of slumber. Upon our slumber, no doubt, there still breaks the occasional voice of a prophet who persists—who bids us arise and get ready for the battle, or flee from the wrath to come, or do anything indeed except acquiesce with a sleepy grunt in the despotism of disaster. It is to fight against disaster and destruction that we were born. Our prophets are those who put wakeful hearts in us for the conflict.

There should perhaps be no prophet needed to belabour us into making an end of such disasters as have recently taken place in so far as they are preventable. Even our common-sense, it might be thought, would be strong enough to insist upon the ordinary rules of caution being observed in ships and railways, and, though most of us are in little danger of dying in a pit explosion, even in coal-mines. Sometimes, when I read the evidence of the cause of a railway disaster, and find a managing director or someone else in authority confessing, without repentance, that his committee for one reason or another ignored the recommendations made by the Board of Trade for the general safety, I marvel that the public never rise up and demand that a railway director shall be hanged. I have small belief in capital punishment, but if capital punishment must still be permitted in order to add a spice to the lives of newspaper readers, then I should confine it to railway directors and other magnates who, though they never commit a murder privately for the delight of the thing, still run a system of murder far more sensational in results than any that was ever planned by French motor-bandits. Think of all the railway accidents of recent times—the accidents of every day to the men on the line, and the accidents of red-letter days to us of the general public. There have been so many of these lately that even the most stupid devotees of private ownership are beginning to think that somebody must be responsible; and if somebody is responsible, then in a society which resorts to penal measures somebody deserves punishment. It is ridiculous to send weak-minded women to gaol for borrowing knicknacks off a shop counter while you send strong-minded railway directors to Belgravia and Mayfair for maintaining a system of sudden death for workmen and travellers. In the days of the Irish famine, coroners' juries, whose business it was to report on the death of some starved man, used to bring in a verdict of wilful murder against Lord John Russell. Is there no coroner's jury of the present day to bring in an occasional verdict of wilful murder against the directors of a railway or a factory? When we see a railway manager sentenced to seven years' penal servitude as the reasonable consequence of some disaster on the line, I have an idea that the number of railway accidents will diminish. When we see the directors of a shipping company fined a year's income and a captain dismissed from his post for sending a ship full steam ahead through a fog, we shall be thrilled by fewer accidents at sea. But it is the old story. One's crime has only to be on a sufficiently grand scale to be as far above punishment as an act of God. What punishment can be too severe for a half-witted farm hand who burns his master's haystack? But as for the railway lords who burn a score of men, women and children in the course of a railway smash by their carefully calculated carelessness, why, one might as well call down punishment on a thunderstorm. It pleases our indolent brains to regard accidents associated with dividends as the works of an inscrutable Providence. It is not enough that Providence should be the author, at least passively, of earthquakes and gales and tidal waves. He must also be held accountable for every breakage of bones that occurs as the result of our passion for saving money rather than life. Some day, I hope, the distinction between Providence and the capitalist will be a little clearer than it at present is. The confusion between the two has hitherto led to the capitalist's being invested with a sacrosanctity to which we offer up human sacrifices on a scale far surpassing anything ever known in Peru or the dark places of Africa.

It would be folly however to prophesy a world from which disaster has disappeared on the heels of the mastodon. One can do little more than regulate disaster. We already regulate death by offering a strong discouragement to murder. Pessimists may contend that, in a world where so many deaths are taking place as it is, one or two more or less can hardly matter. But all the advances the human race has ever made have only been an affair of one or two—the distribution of one or two women, of one or two privileges, of one or two pennies. Consequently, even in a world where disasters grow as thick as trees, we are bound to fight them so far as they can be fought. If we do not, the wilderness will swallow us. One is usually consoled by the leader-writers, after a disaster has taken place, by the reflection that it has taught us certain lessons that will never, never be forgotten. Unfortunately, we knew the lessons already. We do not want to be taught our A B C over again by having the alphabet burned into our flesh with a red-hot iron.

At the same time, the leader-writers do well in trying to arrive at some philosophy of disaster. But the true philosophy of disaster is one which will teach us to rage where raging will be of avail and to endure where there is nothing for it but endurance. Most of us in these days are content to have no philosophy at all, philosophy being a name for serious thought about the universal disaster of death. To read Montaigne, who lived blithely in conversation with death, is to step right out of our modern civilisation into a wiser world. It is to become an inhabitant of the universe instead of a rather inefficient earner of an income. Montaigne tells us that, even when he was in good health, if a thought occurred to him during a walk he jotted it down at once for fear he might be dead before he could reach home and write it down at leisure. He made himself as familiar with death as he was with the sun or his neighbours. He explains what a happiness it would have been to him to write a history of the way in which different great men had died, and his essays are in great part an expression of interest in the caprices of death among the heroes of the human race. History was to him a procession of disasters—disasters, however, seen against a background of faith in the benevolence of the scheme of things—and he made his account with life as something to be enjoyed as a privilege rather than a right.

"If a man could by any means avoid it," he said of death, "though by creeping under a calf's skin, I am one that should not be ashamed of the shift." Somehow, one hardly believes him. He seems here to be speaking for our reassurance rather than historically. On the other hand, he is right a thousand times in summoning even the most timid-kneed to go out and shake hands with disaster as with a friend. To hide from it is only a kind of watered-down atheism. It is a distrust of life. It is easy, of course, to compose sentences on the subject: it is quite another thing to compose ourselves. Matthew Arnold relates in one of his prefaces how he once failed to bring any consolation to the occupants of a railway carriage at a time when a panic about murder in railway trains was running its course by bidding them reflect that, even if any of them died suddenly by violent hands, the gravel-walks of their villas would still be rolled, and there would still be a crowd at the corner of Fenchurch Street. It is a very rational mind that can get comfort out of a thought like that. Even when we are not troubled by thinking of our work or our family, we cannot but cry out against the corruption of this flesh of our bodies, and many of us quake at the thought of the enforced adventure of the soul into a secret world. Marked down for disaster, we may add to our income, or win a place in the Cabinet, or make a reputation for singing comic songs, but death will steal upon us in our security, and strip us bare of everything save the courage we have learned from philosophy and the faith that has been given us by religion. We spend our hours shirking that fact. Cowardice and pessimism will avail on our death-beds no more than wealth or stuffed birds of paradise. Logically, then, every circumstance shouts to us to be brave. But, alas! bravery, though in face of the disasters of others it is easy enough, in the face of our own disasters is a rare and splendid form of genius, To attain it is the crown of existence.

XXII
THE RIGHTS OF MURDER

Mr Justice Darling, before passing a sentence of seven years' penal servitude on Julia Decies for wounding her lover with intent to kill him, made a remark which must interest all students of the morals of murder. No one, probably, he declared, would very much lament the wounded man, but "that was not the question." So far as one can gather from the scrappy reports in the newspapers, the crime was in the main a crime of jealousy. The man and woman had lived together for some years, had then separated, had come back to each other, and had finally quarrelled as the result of a suggestion "that he had taken up with some other woman, with whom he was going to Paris." Incidentally it was stated that the man had given Julia Decies £500 and some furniture in the previous October on the understanding that she was to trouble him no further. It was also stated that "the prosecutor had infected the woman with a terrible disease and that she was pregnant." There you have a story of contemporary life as mean in its horror as any that Gorky has written. It is a story in which the only conceivably beautiful element is the insurgent anger of the woman. It is a tragedy, not of heroic suffering, but of the dull slums of human nature. Probably, in any country where they managed things according to "rough justice" instead of with judges and juries, no one would have blamed Julia Decies even to the extent of a day's imprisonment for seeking to avenge herself in the most extreme form on an environment so intolerable—on a man whom, in the judge's phrase, "no one, probably, would very much lament." There is a mining camp logic which holds that if a man is not worth lamenting, one need not be greatly concerned whether he is alive or dead. Civilisation however, speaking from under the wig of Mr Justice Darling, says of even the most worthless of its human products: "He was a person whose life was entitled to the protection of the law as though he were a person with the best of characters." To the moralist of the mining camp this would seem like saying that the weeds have as good a right to exist as the flowers.

It is obviously one of the earliest instincts of man to get rid of his rivals by killing them. Cain was representative of the human race at this barbarous stage. It is the stage of unhampered egoism, of *laissez-faire* applied to morals. Poets, who sometimes inherit this egoism, have written sympathetically of Cain: now that art is becoming deliberately primitive again, we may expect to see new statues to Cain insolently set up in the poets' back bedrooms. Civilisation is, in one aspect, a war against Cain and the minor poets. It depends in its early stages on the suppression of the private right to murder—on the socialisation, one may say, of the right to kill. No doubt, even in the most highly-developed civilisations, the right to kill is still left to some extent in the hands of private individuals. One has the right to kill certain people in self-defence. But the more advanced civilisation is, the more limited will that right be. So limited has it become in modern England that it has been maintained one is not even entitled to shoot a burglar unless, by running away and in various other ways, one has first exhausted all the gentler devices for escaping injury at his hands. This may seem a sad falling-away from the dramatic virtues of the heroic age, when one slung dead burglars round one's neck like a bag of game. But the heroic age, as has been pointed out, was an age of egoists, not of citizens. When heroes evolved into citizens, as we see in the history of Athens, the culminating triumph came with the abandonment of the right to kill as symbolised in the carrying of arms. Athens was the first city in Greece in which the men went about unarmed. That was a recognition of the fact that civilised man is not a killing animal to the greatest degree possible, but only in the least degree possible.

It may be retorted, on the other hand, that murder was not condoned in the case either of Cain or of Orestes, and there are many other examples of guilty murderers in the heroic age. This, however, only means that there was some limitation put upon the right to kill from the beginning. The right to kill did not exist as against the members of one's own family. It would have been impossible to explain the humour of *The Playboy of the Western World* to men of the heroic age. The women who flocked with their farmhouse gifts to show their appreciation of the boy who had killed his father would have seemed long-nailed monsters of depravity to the Greeks of the time of Œdipus. Professor Freud, in his book on dreams, maintains that men in all ages desire to kill their fathers out of jealousy; he contends even that Hamlet's reluctance to kill his father's murderer was due to the fact that he had often wished to murder his father himself. This, however, is an abnormal interpretation of the jealousies and hatreds of human beings. The philosopher, perhaps, may see the principle of murder in every feeling of anger in the same way as the Christian Apostle saw that, if you hate a man, you are already a murderer in your own heart. The hatred of parents and children, however, is not universal any more than the hatred of husbands and wives. Still, family quarrels are sufficiently natural to enable us to see that the first step towards good citizenship must have been the prohibition of the right to kill the members of one's own family. Gradually, the family widened into the clan, the clan into the city, the city into the nation, the nation into the larger unit embracing men of the same colour, and it will ultimately widen, one hopes, into the human race. But we are far from having reached that stage yet. It is said to be almost impossible to get a death sentence passed on an Englishman who has murdered an Indian native. This merely means that it is regarded as a lesser crime for a European to murder an Asiatic than for a European to murder a European. In other words the family sanctities have been extended in some respects so as to cover Europe, but they have not yet overflowed so far as Asia and Africa. The objection of the war-at-any-price party to-day to civil war is purely on the ground that it is fratricidal—that it is an outrage on recognised family sanctities. The militarists do not see that every war is fratricidal—that every war is a civil war. As a rule, indeed, they deny the existence of family rights outside the borders of their own nation in the narrowest sense. They do not realise that it is as horrible a thing to shoot fellow-Europeans—not to say, fellow-men—as it is to shoot fellow-countrymen. As private citizens they not only admit but insist upon the foreigner's right to live. As public-minded men and patriots, they will admit nothing beyond his right to be carried off on a stretcher if they fail to kill him on the field of battle.

This, however, is to discuss Cain as a statesman rather than Cain as a human being—to consider the social right to kill rather than the individual right to kill. Public morals being so far in the rear of private morals, it raises an entirely different question from that suggested by Mr Justice Darling's remark. Mr Justice Darling laid it down that the private citizen has not—except, it may be presumed, in the last necessities of self-defence—the right to kill even the most worthless and treacherous of human beings. The spy, the sweater, the rack-renter, the ravisher—each has the right to trial by his peers. This, I believe, is good morals as well as good law. Even where it is a case of a blackguard's commission of some unspeakable crime for which there is no legal redress, though we may sympathise with his murderer, we cannot praise the murder. There are, it may be admitted, cases of murder with a high moral purpose. These are especially abundant in the annals of political assassination, which may be described as private murder for public reasons. Very few of us would claim to be the moral equals of Charlotte Corday, and we have abased ourselves for centuries before the at-last-suspected figures of Harmodius and Aristogeiton. There are crimes which are the crimes of saints. Our reverence for the saintliness leads us almost into a reverence for the crime. The hero of Finland a few years ago was a young man who slew a Russian tyrant at the expense of his own life. Deeds like this have the moral glow of self-sacrifice beyond one's own most daring attempts at virtue. How, then, is one to condemn them? But we condemn them by implication if we do not believe in imitating them; and few of us would believe in imitating them to the point of bringing up our children to be even the most honourable of assassins. One unconsciously analyses these crimes into their elements, some of them noble, some of them the reverse. One has heard, again, of what may be called private murders for family reasons—crimes of revenge for some wrong done to a mother, a sister, or a child. Even here, however, one knows that it is against the interests of the State and of the race that we should admit the right to kill. Once allow crimes of indignation, and every indignant man will claim to be a law to himself. It may be that the prohibition of murder—even murder with the best intentions—is in the interests of society rather than of any absolute code of morality. But even so society must set up its own code of morality in self-defence. In practice, of course, it has also the right to distinguish between crimes that are the outcome of a criminal nature, and crimes that are isolated accidents in the lives of otherwise good men and women. Lombroso was opposed to the severe punishment of crimes of passion—crimes which are not likely to be repeated by those who perpetrate them. This, however, is a plea for the consideration of mitigating circumstances, not an assertion that the crime of murder is in any circumstances justifiable.

XXIII
THE HUMOUR OF HOAXES

It was only the other day that Mr G. A. Birmingham gave us a play about a hoax at the expense of an Irish village, in course of which a statue was erected to an imaginary Irish-American General, the aide-de-camp of the Lord-Lieutenant coming down from Dublin to perform the unveiling ceremony. Lady Gregory, it may be remembered, had previously used a similar theme in *The Image*. And now comes the story of yet another statue hoax from Paris. On the whole the Paris joke is the best of the three. It was a stroke of genius to invent a great educationist called Hégésippe Simon. One can hardly blame the members of the Chamber of Deputies for falling to the lure of a name like that. Perhaps they should have been warned by the motto which M. Paul Bérault, of *L'Eclair*, the perpetrator of the hoax, quoted from among the sayings of the "precursor" to whom he wished to erect a centenary statue. "The darkness vanishes when the sun rises" is an aphorism which is almost too good to be true. M. Bérault, however, relying upon the innocence of human nature, sent a circular to a number of senators and deputies opposed to him in politics, announcing that, "thanks to the liberality of a generous donor, the disciples of Hégésippe Simon have at length been able to collect the funds necessary for the erection of a monument which will rescue the precursor's memory from oblivion," and inviting them to become honorary members of a committee to celebrate the event. Despite the fact that he quoted the sentence about the darkness and the sunrise, thirty of the politicians replied that they would be delighted to help in the centenary rejoicings. M. Bérault thereupon published their names with the story of the hoax he had practised on them, and as a result, according to the newspaper correspondents, all Paris has been laughing at the joke, "the good taste of which," adds one of them, "would hardly be relished in England, where other political manners obtain."

With all respect to this patriotic journalist, I am afraid the love of hoaxing and practical joking cannot be limited to the Latin, or even to the Continental races. It is a passion that is as universal as lying, and a good deal older than drinking. It is merely the instinct for lying, indeed, turned to comic account. Christianity, unable to suppress it entirely, had to come to terms with it, and as a result we have one day of the year, the first of April, devoted to the humours of this popular sin. There are many explanations of the origin of All Fools' Day, one of which is that it is a fragmentary memorial of the mock trial of Jesus, and another of which refers it to the belief that it was on the first of April that Noah sent out the dove from the Ark. But the Christian or Hebrew origin of the festival appears to be unlikely in view of the fact that the Hindus have an All Fools' Day of their own, the Huli Festival, on almost exactly the same date. One may take it that it was in origin simply a great natural holiday, on which men enjoyed the license of lying as they enjoy the license of drinking on a Bank Holiday. There is no other sport for which humanity would be more likely to desire the occasional sanction of Church and State than the sport of making fools of our neighbours. We must have fools if we cannot have heroes. Some people, who are enthusiasts for destruction, indeed, would give us fools and knaves in the place of our heroes, and have even an idea that they would be serving some moral end in doing so. It is on an iconoclastic eagerness of one kind or another that nearly all hoaxing and practical joking is based. It consists chiefly in taking somebody down a peg. The boy who used to shout "Wolf!", however, may have been merely an excessively artistic youth who enjoyed watching the varied expressions on the faces of the sweating and disillusioned passersby who ran to his assistance. Obviously, a man's face is a dozen times more interesting to look at when it is crimson with frustrate virtue than when it is placid with thoughts of the price of pigs.

This is not to justify the morality of hoaxing. It is to explain it as an art for art's sake. Murder can, and has, been defended on the same grounds. It is to be feared, however, that few hoaxers or murderers can be named who pursued their hobby in the disinterested spirit of artists. In most cases there is some motive of cruelty or dislike. One would not go to the trouble of murdering and hoaxing people if it did not hurt or vex somebody or other. Those who invent hoaxes are first cousins of the boy who ties kettles or lighted torches to cats' tails. It is the terror of the cat that amuses him. If the cat purred as the instruments of torture were fitted on to it the boy would feel that he had serious cause for complaint. There is, no doubt, a great deal of the cruelty of boys which is experimental rather than malicious—the practice of blowing up frogs, for instance. But, for the most part, it must be admitted, a spice of cruelty is counted a gain in human amusements. This is called thoughtlessness in boys, but it is a deliberate enthusiasm in primitive man, out of which we have to be slowly civilised. There is probably no more popular game with the infancy of the streets than covering a brick with an old hat in the hope that some glorious fool will come along who will kick hat and brick together, and go limping and swearing on his way. One might easily produce a host of similar instances of the humour of the small boy who looks so like an angel and behaves so like a devil. There are, it may be, thousands of small boys who never perpetrated an act of such cheerful malice in their lives. But even they have usually some other outlet for their comic cruelty. The half of comic literature depends upon someone's getting cudgelled or ducked in a well, or subjected to some pain. It is one of the paradoxes of comedy, indeed, that, even when we like the hero of it, we also like to see him hurt and humiliated. We are glad when Don Quixote is beaten to a jelly, and when his teeth are knocked down his throat. We rejoice at every discomfort that befalls poor Parson Adams. Humour, even when it reaches the pitch of genius, has still about it much of the elemental cruelty of the boy who arranges a pin upon the point of which his friend may sit down, or who pulls away a chair and sends someone sprawling.

Hoaxes, at the best, spring from a desire to harry one's neighbour. As a rule, refined men and women have by this time given up the ambition to cause others physical pain, but one still hears of milder annoyances being practised with considerable spirit. It was Theodore Hook, I believe, who originated the practice of hoaxing tradesmen into delivering long caravans of goods at some house or other, to the fury of the householder and the disturbance of traffic. Every now and then the jest is still revived, whereupon everybody condemns it and—laughs at it. That is one of the oddest facts about the hoax as a form of humour. No one has a good word to say for it, and yet everyone who tells you the story of a hoax tells it with a chuckle. Some years ago a young gentleman from one of the Universities palmed himself off on an admiral—was it not?—as the Sultan of Zanzibar, and was entertained as such by the officers on board one of King George's ships. Everybody frowned at the young gentleman's taste, but nobody outside the Navy failed to enjoy the hoax as the best item of the day's news. Similarly, the Köpenick affair set not only all Germany but all Europe laughing. Skill and audacity always delight us for their own sakes; when it is rogueries that are skilful and audacious, they shock us into malicious appreciation. They are adventures standing on their heads. It is difficult not to forgive a clever impostor so long as it is not we on whom he has imposed.

As for the Hégésippe hoax, it may be that there is even an ethical element in our pleasure. Such a hoax as this is a pin stuck in pretentiousness. If it is an imposture, it is an imposture on impostors. One feels that it is good that members of Parliament should be exposed from time to time. Otherwise they might become puffed up. Still, there remains a very good reason why we should oppose a disapproving front to hoaxes of all sorts. We ourselves may be the next victims. Most of us have a Hégésippe Simon in our cupboards. Whether in literature, history, or politics, the human animal is much given to pretending to knowledge that he does not possess. There are some men whom one could inveigle quite easily into a discussion on plays of Shakespeare and Euripides which were never written. I remember how one evening two students concocted a poem beginning with the drivelling line, "I stood upon the rolling of the years," and foisted it on a noisy admirer of Keats as a work of the master. Similarly, in political arguments, one has known a man to invent sayings of Gladstone and Chamberlain without being challenged. This is, of course, not amusing in itself. It becomes amusing only when the other disputants, instead of confessing their ignorance, make a pretence of being acquainted with the invented quotations. It is our dread of appearing ignorant that leads us into the enactment of this kind of lies. We will go to any extreme rather than confess that we have never even heard of Hégésippe Simon. Luckily, Hégésippe Simon happens to be a person who can trip our pretentiousness up. But the senators and deputies who were willing to celebrate the precursor's centenary were probably not humbugs to any greater degree than if they had consented to celebrate the anniversary of Diderot or Rousseau or Alfred de Musset. It is utter imposture, this practice of doing honour to great names which mean less to one than a lump of sugar; and if an end could be put to centenary celebrations in all countries, no great harm would be done to public honesty. On the other hand, most public rejoicings over men of genius would be exceedingly small if all the speeches and applause had to come from the heart without any addition from those who merely like to be in the latest movement. Perhaps the adherents of Hégésippe Simon are necessary in order to make it profitable to be a man of genius at all. They are not only a useful claque, but they pay. That is why even if William Shakespeare, Anatole France, and Bergson are only other and better known names for Hégésippe, it would be madness to destroy such enthusiasm as has gathered round them. M. Bérault, by his light-hearted hoax on his political opponents, has struck at the very roots of popular homage to men of genius.

XXIV
ANATOLE FRANCE

There does not at first glance seem to be any great similarity between Mr Thomas Hardy and M. Anatole France, the latter of whom has come to London to see how enthusiastically Englishmen can dine when they wish to express their feelings about literature. Yet both writers are extraordinarily alike. Each of them is an incarnation of the spirit of pity, of the spirit of irony. Mr Hardy may have more pity than irony and Anatole France may have more irony than pity. I might put it another way and say that Mr Hardy has the tragic spirit of pity while Anatole France has the comic spirit of pity. But each of them is, in his own way, the last word of the nineteenth century on the universe—the century that extinguished the noon of faith and gave us the little star of pity to light up the darkness instead. Each of them is, therefore, a pessimist—Mr Hardy typically British, Anatole France typically French, in his distress. It is as though Mr Hardy spoke out of a rain-cloud; Anatole France out of a cloud of irresponsible lightnings. There, perhaps, you have an eternal symbol of the difference between the Englishman, who takes his irreligion as seriously as his religion, and the Frenchman, who takes his irreligion as smilingly as his *apéritif*.

It is just because he sums up the end of the nineteenth century so well that Anatole France is already in some quarters a declining fashion. He is the victim of a reaction against his century, not of a reaction against his style. He is the last of the true mockers: the twentieth century demands that even its mockers shall be partisans of the coming race. Anatole France does not believe in the coming race. He is willing to join a society for bringing it into existence—he is even a Socialist—but his vision of the world shows him no prospect of Utopias. He is as sure as the writer of *Ecclesiastes* that every blessed—or, rather, cursed—thing is going to happen over and over again. Life is mainly a procession of absurdities in which lovers and theologians and philosophers and collectors of bric-à-brac are the most amusing figures. It is one of the happy paradoxes of human conduct that, in spite of this vision of futilities, Anatole France came forward at the Dreyfus crisis as a man of action, a man who believed that the procession of absurdities could be diverted into a juster road. "Suddenly," as Brandes has said, "he stripped himself of all his scepticism and stood forth, with Voltaire's old blade gleaming in his hand—like Voltaire irresistible by reason of his wit, like him the terrible enemy of the Church, like him the champion of innocence. But, taking a step in advance of Voltaire, France proclaimed himself the friend of the poor in the great political struggle." He even did his best to become a mob-orator for his faith. Since that time he has given his name willingly to the cause of every oppressed class and nation. It is as though he had no hope and only an intermittent spark of faith; but his heart is full of charity.

That somewhere or other a preacher lay hidden in Anatole France might have all along been suspected by observant readers of his works. He is a born fabulist. He drifts readily into fable in everything he writes. And, if his fables do not always walk straight to their moral in their Sunday clothes, that is not because he is not a very earnest moralist at heart, but because his wit and humour continually entice him down by-paths. It is sometimes as though he set out to serve morality and ended by telling an indecent story— as though he knelt down to pray and found himself addressing God in a series of blasphemies. This is the contradiction in his nature which makes him so ineffectual as a propagandist, so effectual as an artist. Ineffectual, one ought to say, perhaps, not as a propagandist so much as a partisan. For he does propagate with the most infectious charm his view of the animal called man, and the need for being tender and not too serious in dealing with him. If he has not preached the brotherhood of man with the missionary fervour of the idealists, he has at least, in accordance with an idealism of his own, preached a brotherhood of the beasts. He never lets himself savagely loose upon his brother-beasts as Swift does. Even in *Penguin Island*, with all its bitterness, he shakes his head rather than his stick at the vicious kennels of men. The truth is, Epicureanism is in his blood. If he could, he would watch the stream of circumstance, as it went by, with the appreciative indifference of the gods. It is only the preacher in his heart that prevents this. Like his own Abbé Coignard, he shares his loyalty between Epicurus and Christ. Henley once described Stevenson as something of the sensualist, and something of the Shorter Catechist. Translated into French, that might serve as a character-sketch of Anatole France.

Originality has been denied to him in some quarters, but, it seems to me, unjustly. One may find something very like this or that aspect of him in Sterne, or Voltaire, or Heine. But in none of them does one find the complete Anatole France, ironist, fabulist, critic, theologian, artist, connoisseur, politician, philosopher, and creator of character. As artist, he is at many points comparable to Sterne. He has the same sentimental background to his wit, the same tenderness in his ridicule, the same incapacity for keeping his jests from scrambling about the very altar, the same almost Christian sensuality. Sterne, of course, is the more innocent writer, because his intellect was not nearly so covetous of experience. Sterne, though in his humanitarianism he occasionally stood in a pulpit above his time, was content for the most part to work as an artist. He could do all the preaching he wanted on Sundays. On week-days my Uncle Toby and Corporal Trim were the only minor prophets he troubled about. Anatole France, on the other hand, is not a preacher by trade. He has no safety-valve of that kind for his moralisings. The consequence is that he has again and again felt himself compelled to ease his mind by adopting the part of the lay preacher we call the journalist. He is in much of his work a Sterne turned journalist—a Sterne flashingly interested in leaving the world better than he found it and other things that grieve the artistic. He might even be described as the greatest living journalist. The Bergeret series of novels are, apart from their artistic excellence, the most supremely delightful examples of modern European journalism. Similarly, when he turned for a too brief space to literary criticism, he proved himself the master of all living men in the art of the literary causerie. The four volumes of *La Vie Littéraire* will, I imagine, survive all but a few of the literary essays of the nineteenth century. They are in a sense only trifles, but what irresistible trifles!

But no criticism would be just which stopped short at the assertion that Anatole France is to some extent a journalist. So was Dickens for that matter, and so, no doubt, was Shakespeare. It is much more important to emphasise the fact that Anatole France is an artist—that he stands at the head of the artists of Europe, indeed, since Tolstoi died. His novels are not the issue of an impartial love of form, like Flaubert's. They are as freakish as the author's personality; they tell only the most interrupted of stories. They might be said in many cases to introduce the Montaigne method into fiction. They are essays portraying a personality rather than novels on a conventional model. They may have a setting amid early Christianity or early Mediævalism; they may disguise themselves as realism or as fairy tales; but the secret passion of them all is the self-revelation of the author—the portraiture of the last of the mockers as he surveys this mouldy world of churches and courtesans. This portrait peeps round the corner at us in nearly every sentence. "Milesian romancers!" cried M. Bergeret. "O shrewd Petronius! O Noël du Fail! O forerunners of Jean de la Fontaine! What apostle was wiser or better than you, who are commonly called good-for-nothing rascals? O benefactors of humanity! You have taught us the true science of life, the kindly scorn of the human race!" There, by implication, you have the ideal portrait of Anatole France himself—the summary of his temper. The kindly scorn of the human race is the basis upon which the Francian Decalogue will be founded. In *Penguin Island* the scorn at times ceases to be entirely kindly. It ceases even to be scorn. It becomes utter despair. But in *Thaïs*, in *Sur la Pierre Blanche*, in *Le Mannequin d'Osier*, with what a comprehending sympathy he despises the human race! How amiably he impales the little creatures, too, and lectures us on the humours of amorousness and quarrelsomeness and heroism in the insect world! Even the French Revolution he sees in *Les Dieux Ont Soif* as a scuffle of insects to be regarded with amusement rather than amazement by the philosopher among his cardboard toys. Not really amusement, of course, but pity disguised as amusement—the pity, too, not of a philosopher in a garden, but of a philosopher always curiously hesitating between the garden and the street.

XXV
THE SEA

It is only now and then, when some great disaster like the sinking of the *Empress of Ireland* occurs, that man recovers his ancient dread of the sea. We have grown comfortably intimate with the sea. We use it as a highway of business and pleasure with as little hesitation as the land. The worst we fear from it is the discomfort of sea-sickness, and we are inclined to treat that half-comically, like a boy's sickness from tobacco. There are still a few persons who are timid of it, as the more civilised among us are timid of forests: they cannot sleep if they are near its dull roar, and they hate, like nagging, the damnable iteration of its waves. For most of us, however, the sea is a domesticated wonder. We pace its shores with as little nervousness as we walk past the bears and lions in the Zoological Gardens. With less nervousness, indeed, for we trust our bodies to the sea in little scoops of wood, and even fling ourselves half-naked into its waters as a luxury—an indulgence bolder than any we allow ourselves with the tamest lions. Let an accident occur, however—let a ship go down or a bather be carried out in the wash of the tide—and something in our bones remembers the old fears of the monster in the waters. We realise suddenly that we who trust the sea are like the people in other lands who live under the fiery mountains that have poured death on their ancestors time and again. We are amazed at the faith of men who rebuild their homes under a volcano, but the sea over which we pass with so smiling a certainty is more restless than a volcano and more clamorous for victims. Originally, man seems to have dreaded all water, whether of springs or of rivers or of the sea, in the idea that it was a dragon's pasture. There is no myth more universal than that of the beast that rises up out of the water and demands as tribute the fairest woman of the earth. Perseus rescued Andromeda from such a monster as this, and it is as the slayer of a water beast that St. George lives in legend, however history may seek to degrade him into a dishonest meat contractor. Not that it was always a maiden who was sacrificed. Probably in the beginning the sea-beast made no distinction of sex among its victims. In many of the legends, we find it claiming men and women indifferently. In the story of Jonah, it demands a male victim, and in many countries to-day there are men who will not rescue anyone from drowning on the ground that if you disappoint the sea of one victim it will sooner or later have you, whether you are male or female, for your pains. These men regard the sea as some men regard God—a beneficent being, if you get on the right side of it. They see it as the home of one who is half-divinity and half-monster, and who, when once his passion for sacrifice has been satisfied, will look on you with a shining face. Hence all these gifts to it of handsome youths and well-born children. Hence the marriage to it of soothing maidens. In the latter case, no doubt, there is also the idea of a magical marriage, which will promote the fertility of water and land. Matthew Arnold's *Forsaken Merman*, if you let the anthropologists get hold of it, will be shown to be but the exquisite echo of some forgotten marriage of the sea.

These superstitions may reasonably enough be considered as for the most part dramatisations of a sense of the sea's insecurity. We have ceased to believe in dragons and mermaids, chiefly because civilisation has built up for us a false sense of security, and you can arrange in any of Cook's branch offices to spend your week-end silent upon a peak in Darien, commanding the best views of the Pacific. We have, as it were, advertised the sea till it seems as innocuous as a patent medicine. We no more expect to be injured by it than to be poisoned at our meals. We have lost both our fears and our wonders, and as we glide through the miraculous places of Ocean we no longer listen for the song of the Sirens, but sit down comfortably to read the latest issue of the Continental edition of the *Daily Mail*. It is a question whether we have lost or gained more by our podgy indifference. Sometimes it seems as if there were a sentence of "Thou fool" hanging over us as we lounge in our deck-chairs. In any case the men who were troubled by the fancy of Scylla and Charybdis, and were conscious of the nearness of Leviathan, and saw without surprise the rising of islands of doom in the sunset went out none the less high-heartedly for their fears. We are sometimes inclined to think that no one ever quite enjoyed the wonders of the sea before the nineteenth century. We have been brought up to believe that all the ancients regarded the sea, with Horace, as the sailor's grave and that that was the end of their emotions concerning it. Even in the eighteenth century, it has been dinned into us, men took so little impartial pleasure in the sea that a novel like *Roderick Random*, though full of nautical adventures, does not contain three sentences in praise of its beauty. This has always seemed to me to be great nonsense. No doubt, men were not so much at their ease with the sea in the old days as they are now. But be sure the terrors of the sea did not stun the ancients into indifference to its beauty any more than the terrors of tragedy stupefy you or me into insensitiveness. There is a sense of all the magnificence of the sea in the cry of Jonah:

All thy billows and thy waves passed over me.
Then I said, I am cast out of thy sight;...
The waters compassed me about, even to the soul:
The depth closed me round about,
The weeds were wrapped about my head.
I went down to the bottoms of the mountains.

There is perhaps more of awe than of the pleasure of the senses in this. It has certainly nothing of the "Oh, for the life of the sailor-lad" jollity of the ballad-concert. But, then, not even the most enthusiastic sea-literature of this sea-ridden time has. Mr Conrad, who has found in the sea a new fatherland—if the phrase is not too anomalous—never approaches it in that mood of flirtation that we get in music-hall songs. He is as conscious of its dreadful mysteries as the author of the *Book of Jonah*, and as aware of its terrors and portents as the mariners of the *Odyssey*. He discovers plenty of humour in the relations of human beings with the sea, but this humour is the merest peering of stars in a night of tragic irony. His ships crash through the tumult of the waves like creatures of doom, even when they triumph as they do under the guidance of the brave. His sea, too, is haunted by invisible terrors, where more ancient sailors dreaded marvels that had shape and bulk. Mr Masefield's love of the sea is to a still greater extent dominated by tragic shadows. There are few gloomier poems in literature than *Dauber* in spite of the philosophy and calm of its close. It is only young men who have never gone farther over the water than for a sail at Southend who think of the sea as consistently a merry place. Not that all sailors set out to sea in the mood of Hamlet. The praise of the sea life that we find in their chanties is the praise of cheerful men. But it is also the praise of men who recognise the risks and treacheries that lurk under the ocean—a place of perils as manifestly as any jungle in the literature of man's adventures and fears. Perhaps it is necessary that the average man should ignore this dreadful quality in the sea: it would otherwise interfere too much with the commerce and the gaiety of nations. And, after all, an ocean liner is from one point of view a retreat from the greater dangers of the streets of London. But the imaginative man cannot be content to regard the sea with this ignorant amiableness. To him every voyage must still be a voyage into the unknown "where tall ships founder and deep death waits." He is no more impudently at home with the sea than was Shakespeare, who, in "Full fathom five thy father lies," wrote the most imaginative poem of the sea in literature. Even Mr Kipling, who has slapped most of the old gods on the back and pressed penny Union Jacks into their hands, writes of the sea as a strange world of fearful things. When he makes the deep-sea cables sing their "song of the English," he aims at conveying the same sense of awe that we get when we read how Jonah went down in the belly of the great fish. Recall how the song of the deep-sea cables begins:

> The wrecks dissolve above us; their dust drops down from
> afar—
> Down to the dark, to the utter dark, where the blind white
> sea-snakes are.
> There is no sound, no echo of sound, in the deserts of the
> deep,
> Or the great grey level plains of ooze where the shell-
> burred cables creep.

Mr Kipling's particularisations of the "blind white sea-snakes" and "level plains of ooze" achieve nothing of the majesty of the far simpler "bottoms of the mountains" in the song of Jonah. But, when we get behind the more vulgar and prosaic phrasing, we see that the mood of Mr Kipling and the Hebrew author is essentially the same.

It is, nevertheless, man's constant dream that he will yet be able to defeat these terrors of the sea. He sees himself with elation as the conqueror of storms, and makes his plans to build a ship that no accident can sink either in a wild sea or a calm. Before the *Titanic* went down many people thought that the great discovery had been made. The *Titanic* went forth like a boast, and perished from one of the few accidents her builders had not provided against, like a victim of Nemesis in a Greek story. After that, we ceased to believe in the unsinkable ship; but we thought at least that, if only ships were furnished with enough boats to hold everyone on board, no ship would ever again sink on a calm night carrying over a thousand human beings to the bottom. Yet the *Empress of Ireland* had apparently boats enough to save every passenger, and now she has gone down with over a thousand dead in shallow water at the mouth of a river which, the *Times* insists, is at least as safe for navigation as the English Channel, and much safer than the Thames. It is as though the great machines we have invented were not machines of safety, but machines of destruction. They have us in their grip as we thought we had the sea in ours. They do but betray us, indeed, in a new manner into an ancient snare—the snare of a power that, like Leviathan,

> Esteemeth iron as straw,
> And brass as rotten wood.

We must, no doubt, go on dreaming that we shall master the sea, and that we shall do it with machines perfectly under our control. But, if we are wise, we shall dream humbly and put off boasting until we are dead and quite sure that the triumph has been ours. It would be inhuman, I admit, never to feel a thrill of satisfaction at man's plodding success in breaking the sea and the air to his uses, in the discovery of fire, in converting the lightning into an illumination for nurseries. But we still perish by fire and flood, by wind and lightning. We use them, but it is at our peril. It is as though we were favoured strangers in the elements, but assuredly we are not conquerors. Mr Wells in *The World Set Free* makes one of his characters in the pride of human invention shake his fist at the sun and cry out, "I'll have you yet." It would have seemed to the Greeks blasphemy, and it still seems folly for man, a hair-pin of flesh half-hidden in trousers, to talk so. There is no victory that man has yet been able to achieve over matter that he does not before long discover has merely delivered him into a new servitude.

XXVI
THE FUTURISTS

The appearance of the first number of *Blast* ought to put an end to the Futurist movement in England. One can forgive a new movement for anything except being tedious: *Blast* is as tedious as an attempt to play Pistol by someone who has no qualification for the part, but whom neither friends nor the family clergyman can persuade into the decency of silence. It may be urged that *Blast* does not represent Futurism, but Vorticism. But, after all, what is Vorticism but Futurism in an English disguise—Futurism, one might call it, bottled in England, and bottled badly? One has only to compare the pictures of the Vorticists recently shown at the Goupil Gallery with the pictures of the Italian Futurists which are being shown at the Doré to see that the two groups differ from each other not in their aims, but in their degrees of competence. No one going through the gallery of Italian paintings and sculpture could fail to see that Boccioni, with all his freakishness, his hideousness, his discordant introduction of real hair, glass eyes, and so forth into his statuary, is an artist powerful both in imagination and in technique. His study of a woman in a balcony is of a kind to bring an added horror into a night of human sacrifices in the Congo. His representation of Matter destroys the appetite like a nightmare that has escaped from the obscene bowels of the sea. It produces, one cannot deny, an emotional effect, like some loathsome and shapeless thing. Compare with it most of the work that is being done in England under Futurist inspiration and you will see the immense difference in mere power. How seldom, apart from the work of Mr Nevinson and one or two others, one finds among the latter a picture that is more interesting to the imagination than a metal toast-rack! You see a picture that looks like a badly opened sardine-tin, and you discover that it is called "Portrait of Mother and Infant." You see another that looks as if someone had taken a pair of scissors and cut a Union Jack into squares and triangles, and had then rearranged the pieces at random in a patchwork quilt, and this, in turn, is labelled, say, "Tennyson reading *In Memoriam* to Queen Victoria." In either case, if the thing were done once, it might be funny. But the young artists are not content to have done it once. They keep on emptying the contents of ragbags and dustbins on to canvases in the most wearisome way. After a time one can neither laugh at them nor take them seriously. One can simply repeat the name of their new review with violent sincerity.

It is not, however, with the Futurists themselves that one's chief quarrel is. It is with the people who do not support the Futurists, but will not condemn them for fear of going down to posterity in the same boat as the people who once ridiculed Wagner and the Impressionists. This fear of the laughter of posterity is surely the last sign of decadence. It is the kind of thing that, in the religious world, would prevent you from criticising the Prophet Dowie or Mrs Eddy. It would compel you to take all new movements seriously simply because they were new. It would lead you to suspend your judgment about the Tango till you were in your grave and your grandchild could come and whisper posterity's verdict to your tombstone. It is, I agree, a fine thing to have a hospitable mind for new things—to be able to greet a Wordsworth or a Manet appreciatively on his first rising. Artists have the right to demand that their work shall be judged, not according to whether it fits in with certain old standards, but by its new power of affecting the emotions and the imagination. Great artists are continually extending the boundaries of their art, and there are, in the last resort, no rules to judge art by except that the artist must by one means or another succeed in bringing something to life. Boccioni satisfies the test in his sculpture, and therefore we must praise him, whether we like his methods or not. The majority of the Futurists, on the other hand, produce no more effect of life than a diagram in Euclid which has been crossed and blotted out with inks of various colours.

Even, however, when, as in the case of the sculptures of Boccioni and the paintings of Severini, we admit that a brilliant imagination is at work, we are not necessarily committed to belief in the methods through which that imagination happens to express itself. It is possible to enjoy Whitman's poetry without believing that he has laid down the essential lines for the poetry of the future. One may agree that Boccioni and Severini have justified their methods by results as far as they themselves are concerned; this does not mean that one agrees with them when they preach the adoption of their methods by artists in general. One takes the Futurist movement seriously, indeed, only because various clever men have joined it, and because young Italians, more than most of us, seem to be justified in some form of violent reaction against a past that oppresses them. Whether Futurism is merely the growing pains of a rejuvenated Italy, or whether it is a genuine manifestation of the old passion for violence which first showed itself on the day on which Cain killed Abel, it is difficult at times to say. Probably it is a little of both. "We wish," says Marinetti, praising violence like any Prussian, in a famous manifesto, "to glorify war—the only health-giver of the world—militarism, patriotism, the destructive aim of the Anarchist, the beautiful ideas that kill, the contempt for women." And, again: "We shall extol aggressive movement, feverish insomnia, the double quickstep, the somersault, the box on the ear, the fisticuff." It is very like Mr Kipling at the age of fourteen writing for a school magazine, if you could imagine a Kipling emancipated from religion and belief in British law and order. Later, as Marinetti proceeds to foretell the day on which the Futurists shall be slain by their still more Futuristic successors, the schoolboy wakes once more in him. "And Injustice, strong and healthy," he writes,—how one envies the fine flourish with which he does it!—"will burst forth radiantly in their eyes. For art can be naught but violence, cruelty, and injustice." One need not be too solemn with writing like that. It may be growing pains, or it may be a new jingoism of the individual, but, whichever it is, it is amusing nonsense. One begins to swear only when people above the school age insist upon taking it seriously as though it might contain a new gospel for humanity. It contains no new gospel at all. It is merely an entertaining restatement of an egoism of a kind that man was trying to discard before the days of bows and arrows. It is a schoolboyish plea for the revival of the tomahawk. It is a war-song played in a city street on the bottom of a tin can. It has no more to do with art than a display of penny fireworks, an imitation of barking dogs at the calves of old gentlemen, or the escapades of Valentine Vox. It has no relation to art whatsoever except from the fact that Marinetti himself is an exceedingly clever writer, as one may see from almost any of his manifestoes. One may turn for an example of his manner to the following passage from his summons to the young to destroy the museums, the libraries, and the academies ("those cemeteries of wasted efforts, those calvaries of crucified dreams, those ledgers of broken attempts!"):

Come, then, the good incendiaries with their charred fingers!... Here they come! Here they come!... Set fire to the shelves of the libraries! Deviate the course of canals to flood the cellars of the museums!... Oh! may the glorious canvases drift helplessly! Seize pick-axes and hammers! Sap the foundations of the venerable cities!

The oldest amongst us is thirty; we have, therefore, ten years at least to accomplish our task. When we are forty, let others, younger and more valiant, throw us into the basket like useless manuscripts!... They will come against us from afar, from everywhere, bounding upon the lightsome measure of their first poems, scratching the air with their hooked fingers, and scenting at the academy doors the pleasant odour of our rotting minds, marked out already for the catacombs of the libraries.

That is a vivid piece of humour. It is as amusing as Marinetti's portrait of himself at the Doré Gallery—a portrait the head of which is a clothes brush and the hat a tobacco tin—a toy which would be in its right place, not at an exhibition of paintings, and sculpture, but in the nursery squares of Mrs Bland's Magic City.

As a matter of fact, however, Futurism as an artistic method seems to have only the slightest connection with Marinetti's neo-Zarathustraisms. The Futurist painters give us, not the blood that Marinetti calls for, but diagrams as free from implications of bloodshed as a weather-chart or the illustrations in an engineering journal. These artists are not primarily concerned with protesting against the conversion of Italy into a "market for second-hand dealers." They aim at inventing a new kind of art which shall be able to paint, not objects in terms of form and colour, but the movements of objects and the states of mind of those who see them. They have invented a jargon about "simultaneousness," "dynamism," "ambience," and so forth, which is about as impressive as the writings of Mrs Eddy; and they paint in the same jargon in which they write. "Paint the soul, never mind the legs and arms," recommended the cleric in *Fra Lippo Lippi*. "Paint the simultaneousness, never mind the legs and arms," is the golden rule of the Futurists. They have conceived a strange contempt for the visible world. They tell us that a running horse "has not four legs, but twenty," but that is no reason for leaving the horse entirely out of the picture, as some of the enthusiasts do. They do not realise that our sensations about horse and the movements of horse can only be painted in terms of horse—that art is not a dissipation of life into wavy lines and dots and dashes, but the opposite. There may be a science of Futurism in which the "force-lines" of a horse or a motor car may be part of a useful diagram. These arbitrary lines, however, have no more to do with imaginative art than the plus and minus signs in arithmetic. Occasionally, of course, there is an obvious symbolism in the lines as in the charging angles which represent the dynamism of a motor car. But this is merely speed expressed by a commonplace symbol instead of by a symbolic impression of the flying car itself. This is an intellectual game rather than an art. Occasionally it gives us a wonderful piece of broken impressionism; but the stricter Futurists are symbolistic beyond all understanding. Their work is like an allegory, to the meaning of which one has no key—an allegory printed in the hieroglyphs of an unknown language.

XXVII
A DEFENCE OF CRITICS

Mr E. F. Benson has been attacking the critics, and reviving against them the old accusation that they are merely men who have failed in the arts. There could scarcely be a more unsupported theory. As a matter of fact, to take Mr Benson's own art, there are probably far more bad critics who end as novelists than bad novelists who end as critics. Criticism is usually the beginning, and not the decadence, of a man's authorship. Young men nowadays criticise before they graduate. One becomes a critic when one puts on long trousers. It is as natural as writing poetry. Indeed, the gift seems in some ways to be related to poetry. It springs at its best from the same well of imagination. This is not to compare the art of the critic to the art of the poet in importance, but only in kind. Criticism is by its nature bound to keep closer to the earth than poetry. It has frequently more resemblance to the hedge-sparrow than to the lark. It is a chatterbox of argument, not a divine spendthrift of the beauty that is above argument. It is the interpreter of an interpretation. It gives us beauty second-hand. Critics are compared somewhere to "brushers of noblemen's clothes." In an honest world, however, one might brush a nobleman's clothes not out of servility, but out of tidiness. There would have been nothing degrading in it if Queen Elizabeth herself had ironed the stains out of Shakespeare's doublet, provided she had done it from decent motives. Critics of the better sort need not worry when their service is misconstrued as servitude. Those who attack them are usually men who are under the delusion that it is better to be a bad artist than a good critic. Thus we find the author of *Lanky Bill and His Dog Bluebeard* looking down with patronage on a man like Hazlitt, because he lacked something that is called the creative gift. Even the life and work of Walter Pater have not succeeded in dispelling the popular notion that the imagination is more honourably employed in inventing sentences for sawdust figures than in relating the experiences of one's own soul. According to this standard, Mr Charles Garvice must be ranked higher among imaginative authors than Sir Thomas Browne, and the *Essays of Elia* must give place to the novels of Mrs Florence Barclay. Clearly no line can be drawn on principles of this kind between imaginative and unimaginative literature. The artists, for the most part, are as lacking in imagination as the critics. They have merely chosen a more luxurious form of writing. Oscar Wilde used to say that anybody could make history, but only a man of genius could write it; and one might contend in the same way that nearly anybody can make literature, but only a clever man can criticise it. The genius of the critic is as much an original gift as the genius of a runner or a composer.

One need not go back further than Dryden to realise to what an extent the successful artists have thrown themselves into the work of criticism. Most of us nowadays find Dryden's prefaces and his *Essay on Dramatic Poesy* easier reading than his verse; and, in the age that followed, criticism seems to have come as naturally to the men of letters as conversation. Addison, commonplace critic though he was, was always airing his views on poetry and music; and what is Pope's *Dunciad* but a comic epic of criticism? Nor was Dr Johnson less concerned with thumping the cushion in the matter of literature than in the matter of morals. His *Lives of the Poets* does not seem a great book to us who have been brought up on the romantic criticism of the nineteenth century, but it is an infinitely better book than *Rasselas*, which has the single advantage that it is shorter. And so one might go on through the list of great men of letters from Johnson's to our own day. Burke, Scott, Coleridge, Wordsworth, Macaulay, Carlyle, Thackeray, Ruskin, Matthew Arnold, Swinburne, Pater, Meredith, Stevenson—I choose more or less at a hazard a list of imaginative writers who are in the very midstream of English criticism. Even in our own day, how many of the poets and novelists have graduated as critics! What lover of Mr Henry James is there who would not almost be willing to sacrifice one of his novels rather than his *Partial Portraits*? Who is there, even among Mr Bernard Shaw's detractors, who would wish his dramatic criticisms unwritten? And who would not exchange a great deal of Mr George Moore's fiction for another book like *Impressions and Opinions*? Similarly, Mr W. B. Yeats has revealed his genius in a book of criticism like *Ideas of Good and Evil* no less than in a book of verse like *The Wind among the Reeds*; Mr William Watson's works include a volume of *Excursions in Criticism*; Sir Arthur Quiller-Couch has published two volumes of critical causeries; Mr Max Beerbohm is no less distinguished as a critic than as a caricaturist; "A. E." reviews books in *The Irish Times*, and Mr Walter De la Mare in *The Westminster Gazette*. Here surely is a list that may suggest a doubt in the minds of those who take the view that the critics are merely a mob of embittered hacks who have failed at everything else. This is one of those traditional fallacies, like the stage Irishman, which men accept apparently for the sake of ease. Even the most superficial enquiries at the offices of the newspapers and the weekly reviews would reveal the fact that a great percentage of the best poets and novelists either are engaged, or have been engaged in their green and generous days, in the work of criticism. If Shakespeare were alive to-day he would probably earn his living at first, not by holding horses' heads, but by turning dramatic critic. Every artist worth his salt has in him the makings of a journalist. Milton himself was as ferocious a pamphleteer as any of those blood-and-thunder rectors whom we see quoted by "Sub Rosa" in *The Daily News*. Tolstoy was as furiously active, if not so furiously bitter, a journalist. And who is the most charming and graceful journalist and critic of our own day but the charming and graceful novelist, Anatole France?

All this, however, is no reply to Mr Benson's indictment of the critics on the ground that they do not discover genius, but that the public has to discover genius in spite of them. It is one of those indictments which can only be believed on the assumption that the critics are a race apart who think, as it were, *en masse*. Those who repeat it seem to regard the critics as a disciplined army of destruction instead of realising that they are a hopelessly straggling company of more or less ordinary men and women of varying tastes, with a sprinkling of men and women of genius among them. They tell us that the critics attacked the Pre-Raphaelites, but they forget that Ruskin was a critic and a prophet of the Pre-Raphaelites. They tell us that the critics cold-shouldered Browning; but W. J. Fox wrote enthusiastically of Browning almost from the first, and Pater praised him in his early essays: it was a poet who, alas! was not a critic—Tennyson—who said the severest things about him. Ibsen, again, is constantly cited as an example of an artist who had to make his way to public acceptance through mobs of shrieking critics. But what do we find to be the case? In England three of the most remarkable critics of their time, Mr Bernard Shaw, Mr Edmund Gosse, and Mr William Archer, fought a desperate fight for Ibsen against almost the entire British public. The critics who attacked Ibsen did not represent the flower of British criticism, but the flower of the British public. It will be found, I believe, to be an almost invariable rule that whenever the critics have attacked men of genius, they have had the public at their back cheering them on. There are critics, indeed, who make themselves into the hired mouthpieces of the public. They long to express not what they themselves think (for they do not think), but what the public thinks (though it does not think). Can Mr Benson point to any notable catch of genius ever made by critics of this kind? I do not, of course, contend that even the most intelligent reviewer in these days, (who is one of the most hard-worked of journalists), is in a good position for discovering new stars of genius. No man can appreciate a Shakespeare that is thrown at his head, and books are thrown at the heads of reviewers nowadays in numbers likely to stun or bewilder rather than to evoke the mood of rapturous understanding. As for the reviewers, they are as varied a crowd as the rest of the public. One of them enjoys *The Scarlet Pimpernel* better than Shakespeare; another blames Miss Marie Corelli for not writing like Donne; another has read and rather liked Shelley. On the whole, they are fonder of good books than most people. They have to read so many bad books as a duty, that many of them ultimately get a taste for literature as a blessed relief. But, as for attacking men of genius, why, nine out of ten of them would not attack a mouse, unless the prejudices of the public they reverence drove them to it. They are very nice and affable, like the gentleman in *You Never Can Tell*—the nicest and most affable set of human beings that ever manufactured butter outside a dairy.

XXVIII
ON THE BEAUTY OF STATISTICS

One of the most unexpected pages in Sir Edward Cook's *Life of Florence Nightingale,* is that in which he describes Miss Nightingale, in a phrase Lord Goschen once used about himself, as a "passionate statistician." Somehow one did not associate statistics with Florence Nightingale. She had already taken her place in the sentimental history of the world as the angel of the wounded soldier. It is a disturbance to one's preconceptions to be asked to regard her as the angel among the Blue Books. As Sir Edward Cook reveals her to us, however, she is ardent in the pursuit of figures as other women in pursuit of a figure. We read how she helped one of the General Secretaries of the International Statistical Congress of 1860 to draw up the programme for the section dealing with sanitary statistics, at which, indeed, her own pet scheme for uniform hospital statistics was the chief subject of discussion. Her faith in statistics, however, went far beyond that of statistical congresses. She believed that statistics were in a measure the voice of God. "The laws of God were the laws of life, and these were ascertainable by careful, and especially by statistical, inquiry." That is how Sir Edward Cook explains his remark that her passion for statistics was "even a religious passion."

It is by no means to be wondered at that the religion of statistics made its appearance in the nineteenth century. The surprising thing is, that no church has yet been founded in its honour. In the history of religion, philosophy and magic, numbers have again and again played a leading part; and what are statistics but numbers on regimental parade? Pythagoras found in number the ultimate principle of creation. Xenocrates went a step farther when he defined the soul as "a number which moves itself." To the unphilosophical reader the definition of Xenocrates is the merest riddle till one realises that he was probably trying to destroy the idea that the soul was something material, a fact of space, as might be connoted by words like "thing" or "living being." This is why, in order to express the soul, it was necessary to use an abstraction; and what so abstract as number? Nor did the numerical explanation of the universe stop here. "Pure reason," Gomperz tells us, in speaking of the Pythagoreans in *Greek Thinkers,* "was assimilated to unity, knowledge to duality, opinion to triplicity, sense-perception to quadruplicity." What a jargon it all seems—a game of the intellect! But the heavenly arithmetic has lingered in the world to our own day, and among simple people, too.

The mystery of numbers has entered into folklore as well as into philosophy, as that fine jingle, "Green grow the rushes, O!" which survives in half a dozen English counties, shows. It has always seemed to me the perfect expression of the fantastic lyricism of numbers:

> I'll sing you one O!
> Green grow the rushes O!
> What is your one O?

And so on till we reach the number twelve in the catalogue of holy delights:

> Twelve are the twelve apostles;
> Eleven, eleven went up to heaven;
> Ten are the ten commandments;
> Nine are the bright shiners;
> Eight are the bold rainers:
> Seven, seven are the stars in heaven;
> Six are the proud walkers;
> Five are the symbols at your door;
> Four are the gospelmakers;
> Three, three is the rivals;
> Two, two is the lilywhite boys,
> Clothed all in green, O!
> One is one and all alone
> And ever more shall be so.

What it all means is for the folklorists to dispute about. It is interesting in the present connection chiefly as the ruins of an arithmetical statement of the mysteries of the universe. Similar chants of number are known in all religions. They are common to Christianity, Mohammedanism and Judaism. One is told that, on the night of the Passover, Jewish families chant a list of numbers, beginning "Who knoweth One?" and going on to "Who knoweth thirteen?" with its answer:

> I, saith Israel, know thirteen: Thirteen divine attributes—twelve tribes—eleven stars—ten commandments—nine months preceding childbirth—eight days preceding circumcision—seven days of the week—six books of the Mishnah—five books of the Law—four matrons—three patriarchs—two tables of the covenant—but One is our God, who is over the heavens and the earth.

This list may be regarded as a mere aid to memory, and no doubt it is to some extent that. But it is also an example of the religious use of numbers—a use which has given various numbers a magic significance. One has an example of this magic significance in the custom, among those who resort to holy wells, of walking round the well nine times in the opposite direction to the sun. One always has to do things by threes or sevens or nines. Similarly, the belief in the maleficent power of thirteen is commoner in London than in Patagonia, where, indeed, they do not know how to count up to thirteen. One remembers, too, how in recent years the prophetic sort of evangelical Christians were on the look out for some great statesman or conqueror upon whom they could fix the dreaded number of the Antichrist, 666. First it was Napoleon; later it was Gladstone, the letters of whose name, if you slightly misspelt it in Greek, stood for numbers which added up to the awful total. I recall the relief with which in my own childhood I discovered the fact that, however wrongly my name was spelt, and in whatever language, it was not possible to work out 666 as the answer.

So much for the mysteries of numbers. To most people the whole thing will appear a chronicle of superstitions, as astrology does. But, just as astronomy has taken the place of the superstitions of the stars, so statistics has taken the place of the superstitions of numbers. It is as though men had suspected all along that stars and numbers had some significance beyond their immediate use and beauty, but for hundreds of years they could only guess what it was. It was not till the eighteenth century indeed that the science of statistics was discovered—under its present name, at least—and ever since then men have been debating whether it is a science or only a method. Whichever you prefer to call it, it may be described as an explanation of human society in terms of number. It is the discovery of the most efficient symbols that have yet been invented for the realistic portraiture of men in the mass. Symbols, I say advisedly, for statistics is more closely allied to Oriental than to Western art in that it avoids the direct imitation of life and appeals to the imagination through conventional figures. Perhaps it is a certain suspicion of Orientalism that accounts for the fanatical hatred of statistics which still exists among many of the apostles of the West. For statistics is a new thing which has had to fight as desperately for recognition as Impressionist art or Wagnerian opera. Infuriated Victorians still speak of "lies, damned lies, and statistics," as the three degrees of wickedness; and the statistician is denounced in superlatives as a sort of gaoler of humanity, who would give us all numbers instead of names. Now, I am not concerned to defend bad statisticians any more than bad artists. Statistics has its charlatans, its bounders after a new thing, as well as its Da Vincis and its Michelangelos. Or, perhaps it is more comparable to music than to painting or sculpture. The philosophy of number is the philosophy of proportion, of harmony, of rhythm, and statistics is the study of the proportions, harmonies, rhythms of society. Music and poetry, it should be remembered, are both an affair of number. "I lisped in numbers," said the poet, "for the numbers came." And the statistician has the same apology. Statistics, of course, is largely concerned, like the arts, with the disharmonies of life, but it deals with them in terms of harmony. It is a method of asserting order amid chaos, and that is why the lovers of chaos attempt to spread the idea among the people that statistics is a dangerous innovation, a black-coated tyranny. That is why landlords who benefit by the social chaos have fought so hard against the valuation of land, and churches against the registration of ecclesiastical property. Similarly, there was a middle-class party that denounced the income tax because it would mean a statistical inquest into the wealth of manufacturers and shopkeepers. Among savage tribes, we are told, it is a common custom to hide one's name, because those who know one's name have a magic power over one's soul. Similarly, in civilised societies, the rich man likes to hide his number. He knows that in some way the knowledge of this will give society a new control over him. It is possible to ignore all the evils of monopolised riches till one knows the numbers of the rich. To many people it is a turning-point in social and political belief to discover such a fact as that, of the total income of Great Britain and Ireland in 1908,

5,500,000 people received £909,000,000,

while

39,000,000 people received £935,000,000.

In other words, the fact that one-half of the wealth of Great Britain and Ireland goes to the twelve per cent. of the population who belong to the class with incomes over £160 a year. It is a terrible revelation both of poverty and of riches. The figures thunder at one's imagination more effectively than a sea of rhetoric. And the figures concerning destitution and the housing of the poor are still more terrible in their realism. Shelley never wrote a revolutionary hymn that more surely prophesied the coming of a new society. Social greed, that has withstood ten thousand prophets and poets, at last begins to feel troubled in the unaccustomed presence of the statistician. Not the statistician in his study, of course: he is no more than a dryasdust inventor. But the statistician, like Florence Nightingale, with the genius of a fine purpose and a sure aim with sure facts. This is not to discredit any of the old battalions of reform. It is merely to hail the coming of the new regiment of the statisticians, who fight with tables instead of swords, and whose leaders exhort them on the eve of battle with passages out of Blue Books. Statistics and the man I sing. Let the next great epic be an Arithmiad.